Simon Linter

How I Learnt to Stop Missing England and Love the Herring

or

I0540701

A Decade in Sweden

SPLINTER PUBLISHINGS

First published ebook 2013 by BookBaby

First published in paperback 2015 by Splinter Publishings

This edition first published 2015 by Splinter Publishings
Splinter Publishings, Sweden.
www.splinterpublishings.com

ISBN: 978-91-982368-2-8

Printed by Book Printing UK
Remus House, Coltsfoot Drive, Peterborough, PE2 9BF

FSC

Ingen fara på taket

Contents

An introduction 1

Animals 5

Entertainment 17

Language 35

Education 61

Work 73

Music 89

Food & Drink 99

Shopping 129

Housing & Living 145

Society...159

Politics...205

Sport & Fitness 211

Travel, Holidays & Tourists 227

West vs. East 253

Country & Environment 263

Conclusion 275

Appendix (Dictionary & Translations) 279

An introduction

My life began in the up and coming town of Northampton in 1975. My parents had made the move from London to avoid the gazumping in the property market and they were certain that Northampton, nicknamed "shoe town", would fulfill everything they could wish for. For a while, Northampton sufficed. My dad found a decent job and my parents had moved to a new area with nice neighbours. Everything was hunky dory. During my development from childhood to adulthood, I stayed in this up and coming area for quite some time, until I made the move to the town centre when I was 22 years old.

After living in Northampton for such a long time, I had become accustomed to how it worked, how it operated and thought that it was a nice town to live in. I always reacted when outsiders to the town dared to criticise it for being boring and simply crap. Ok, I knew it wasn't the best place to live but I knew it certainly wasn't the worst... ... or was it?

After a short holiday to Gothenburg in 2002, I quickly noticed the differences between this Swedish city and my hometown. It had the advantage of being on the coast, it had a canal going through it, and it only took a short journey to see some really fantastic scenery. I was spoilt by the amount of beauty it had to offer. By the time the holiday had finished, and I had made the journey back to Northampton, I was starting to side with the outsiders that had called Northampton crap. It really didn't have the same friendly laid-back feel that Gothenburg had, and it certainly didn't have the sea as a neighbour. It had a shoe museum that could be walked through in roughly five minutes that profiled the town as the main centre for cobblers in olden times.

In 2003, I handed in my notice at the newspaper where I worked, which raised some questions from my work colleagues:

"You are leaving us? That's a shame. Where are you going to next?"

This was the usual line of questioning as if they were expecting an answer that I had found another newspaper or magazine to work for instead, but my answer was:

"I'm moving actually."

"Oh? To London?"

"Sweden."

"What?"

It was a strange concept to people who assumed I was moving out of Northampton to another town, not out of the UK completely. I was moving for the best reason - love. It's the reason most Brits will move to Sweden with a select few moving just for the hell of it.

I am just one of many Brits who has moved to Sweden who didn't really know what awaited them when they got there. Could I actually survive at all? Would I get a job? Would I ever speak the lingo? Was it obligatory for me to use a sauna naked and eat raw fish at the same time?

All of these questions and more are answered in this book. Now that I have lived in Sweden for ten years, it feels right to write a book like this one.

Most of this book is focused on the comparisons between living in the UK and Sweden, highlighting differences between them. For example, how do ID cards work in Sweden compared to the UK that scrapped them? Why does the wildlife in Sweden display attitude problems compared to the UK wildlife that runs away scared? Why do Swedes feel burdened to owe someone money when they have been bought a drink? It's questions like these that will be answered definitively in this book and it will try to explain why.

If you are an immigrant to Sweden, there are doubtless experiences that I have had that might be similar to yours. This book is my own personal opinion about these experiences and how I handled them. Whatever your reasons are for reading this book, just relax over a cup of coffee, tea if you are British, and just have a giggle, maybe a chuckle, or maybe a full blown laugh attack at what I have found out in a decade living in the country that loves cold fish, Sweden.

1. ANIMALS

You can't help but notice the permanent affection that Swedes have with animals. Just a walk through a city and you'll notice caricatures of elks and reindeer turned into tempting cheap souvenirs for tourists. It's not the stuffed souvenir animal that I want to talk about here; I want to talk about animals that seem to have attitude problems.

THE BIRDS

Back in the UK, my parents are proud of their garden. They mow the lawn when they can, buy new plants, fold up and unfold the washing line, scare off the neighbour's cat and last, but not least, feed the wildlife that consists of birds. My parents buy assorted seeds for the occasion, plonk them outside on a saucer in their garden, sit quietly in their kitchen and wait for the impending bird action. After a short while, the birds descend on the seedy victims, keeping one eye on them whilst keeping one eye on anything else that might want to attack them. The show will be going fine until somebody, usually my dad, barges his way into the kitchen to make a cuppa. The beady, watchful eye of one bird will see the blurry outline of my dad through the window and through the net curtain. After this has happened, there is no turning back. That solitary bird will sound the alarm for the rest of the gang, making them fly away quicker than they had landed. A lengthy thirty minute wait will ensue before they come back again.

This doesn't happen in Sweden. The wildlife seems to have adapted a "whatever" attitude and will stand their ground regardless of what happens. Take for example the humble magpie that is rarely seen in England but seen aplenty in Sweden. You may be walking down a path and spot a magpie seemingly pecking at nothing only for it to look up at you, slowly hop out of the way and then look at you again as if to say:

There! I have hopped out of the way. I hope you are satisfied!

Compare this to England and the bird would have relieved itself of those half digested seeds, flown away and be safely looking at you from a tree before you had got anywhere near it. The same sparrows that fly away at the twitch of an eyebrow in the UK certainly have no fear of man at all in Sweden. The Swedish sparrow is perfectly at ease in landing by your feet, looking up at you and your sandwich, and will wait expectantly for a few breadcrumb donations. The chances of this happening in the UK are zero and the only bird that will approach you in the same fashion is the pigeon. Seagulls, however, bypass waiting by your feet altogether and have instead, chosen to just dive-bomb you and snatch the sandwich from your hands. They've taken out the middleman of the waiting game and cut to the chase when it comes to the art of crumb begging. Swedish seagulls are the hit men of the sandwich-stealing world and will stop at nothing to get the prize.

THE DEER

The "whatever" attitude doesn't stop with airborne sandwich stealers, it is also applicable to land mammals such as deer. Again, when compared to the UK, you would be eating the dust of a deer before you got within an English mile of it (I say English mile because a Swedish mile is different... I'll explain later). A Swedish deer, on the other hand, has absolutely no problem that you are watching it while it tramples through your garden towards your prize-winning roses. The roses, that you nurtured from a seed to buds to beautiful blooming reddy petally visions of delight, are now lunch to a deer that you can't scare away. The Swedish deer has complete disregard towards the fact that you might be in your garden holding a stick, threatening to use it. In fact, the Swedish deer will be in your garden quicker before you can say "get out of it" and making wooden spoon nominees out of those roses you so carefully pruned. There seems to be no explanation to why this attitude has afflicted the usual skitty, cowardly UK deer. I can only assume that they have spoken with the magpies and have all come to the conclusion that Swedes really aren't dangerous.

That is unless the Swede is driving a car...

THE ELK

It has been reported that one of the hazards in certain areas of Sweden has been the much-loved elk, an almost national symbol the country that is used all the time to make money out of German tourists. The elk may be lovable but they certainly don't move very fast and tend not to move at all when faced with a motorist's headlights beaming straight at it. Accidents involving elks usually happen on country lanes and at night, and nobody emerges the winner. The elk usually ends up dying of injuries caused by the car, and the antlers going through the windshield will usually kill the driver. You really have to hope that the elk hasn't spoken to any magpies or deer because if they have, they won't be very happy when they find out their advice of adapting a whatever attitude will get them killed. Imagine, if you will, an elk that is slowly plodding up a road, spots a car heading towards it and thinks to itself:

Pfff. It's my road. By the power of my antlers, be gone car. *CRASH!* Ah crap! Well, that's the last time I talk to a deer.

The elk has become such a serious problem that the Swedish driving test has had to dedicate some time in dealing with them when driving. The school of thought on how to tackle an elk on the road is to aim for the back legs instead of veering off the road or hitting the beast head on. This way, you'll survive and the elk will probably end up as road kill. This is, of course, providing that the elk is not looking at you head on, and then it would be my guess that you would have to swerve around it and then aim for the rear end. It's not a nice thought, but it makes me wonder how the Swedish driving test really prepares people for this encounter. Do they make cardboard elks and draw targets on them? And I thought parallel parking was hard.

Of course, if you believe the stories that surround elks, you'd probably be assuming that they were actually pretty smart. Take, for example, the story or urban myth, of the elk that took a wrong turn in the forest and ended up in the middle of a city. The story has it that the elk smashed through the front window of a bar, found a vacant bar stool, ordered a drink and stayed there the whole night. I can now reveal that this story has been misreported and is, of course, completely wrong. The elk actually didn't want anything to drink and just ordered a packet of peanuts.

The humble elk is also widely reported to be the apple of many German tourists' eyes, providing the deer hasn't eaten the apple. German tourists have been known to walk slowly through forests, with forensic like precision, collecting elk poo. You would think that the poo is collected for agricultural purposes because it contains some magic fertilising component that produces those prize-winning roses. Alas, this isn't the reason. Elk poo is a one of the best selling souvenirs and some tourists can't get enough of the highly prized excrement. If the hooves were on the other feet, would the elks collect human poo and try to sell it at tacky souvenir shops in towns and cities? The jury is out on the answer to the question but I would expect it to be no.

THE BEAR

Although I can't comment on how wild wolves and bears act in their natural Swedish habitat, I can tell you about an experience with a bear at Skansen park in Stockholm. As a tourist at the time, I wanted to take a good photograph of a bear that had unfortunately just eaten its dinner a good half an hour beforehand. Just as I was about to take the shot of a lifetime, the shot that could have been used in National Geographic's magazine, the bear decided to strike a crouching pose to relieve itself. As I moaned out loud about the forthcoming blessing for the ground, the bear looked at me with a pained, almost human like expression as if to say,

Look mate, I'm going to the toilet! Come back later!

Now I can't credit this to the "whatever" attitude because a bear really doesn't need to have a "whatever" attitude, but it was certainly something that can't be easily explained away. If the bear was really that irritated by my attempts to take a photograph of it, then it could have roared at me with claws and teeth being loosely snarled in my direction. Instead, it chose to go with a more pitiful and distressed human approach to the situation. Bizarre indeed!

THE JELLYFISH

Moving on from defecating bears, I didn't want to leave marine life out of the equation. Now I know what you are thinking here. Surely Sweden can't have fish that have a "whatever" attitude too, can they? As we all know, fish would have trouble communicating to the tough magpies, and the deer would just probably try to eat them if they tried to converse with them. No. Instead, I want to talk about the jelly variety of fish that can be found in plentiful supply off the west coast.

I remember being pleased with myself when I spotted a jellyfish for the first time and I was quick to point it out to my girlfriend who just gave a wry smile. It was hard to really figure out why such a smile was being given, but after I had spotted another jellyfish and then another and then another, I understood why. The whole stretch of the sea was full with jellyfish as far as the eye could see. The only other type of jellyfish I had seen before were dead ones that had unfortunately ended up on the shores of Cromer in the UK. I quickly learnt that the white jellyfish were harmless whilst the horrible ones that looked like tufts of floating grass were the ones that burnt you. The boat trip to the island Vargö off the coast of Gothenburg, was reportedly a great place to swim. So, having been informed of stinging jelly-fish in the water, it was something that made my skin quake in fear. My girlfriend reassured me that it was perfectly ok to swim in the waters and that if I saw the yellowy, tufty grassy jellyfish type, it was best to just swim casually away from it.

However, as I was swimming casually away in a panic from a jellyfish that could turn my skin red, I encountered one of the more sociable varieties. The white jellyfish is a harmless, rubbery creature that has unfortunately become a bit of play toy to Swedish children. To any Swedes reading this—hands up those of you who had jellyfish fights with these innocent floating amiable sea life. That many, hmm? It's true. Most Swedes that I have asked seemed to have had a jellyfish fight at some point in their childhood, fishing the poor buggers out of the sea and throwing them at each other. It's probably not the way the white jellyfish envisaged ending up, flying through the air, aimed at some kid's head but what can it do if it can't burn like its evil counterpart?

THE SNAKE

If burning jellyfish has put you off taking a dip then don't worry! Why not take a nature walk through a forest instead where nothing can surely burn you, apart from getting too close to a camp fire. My calm introduction is about to get uncomfortable because I have to mention snakes here. Although Sweden only has one type of poisonous ankle biter, the most common encounter will be with a snake called snok, a type of grass snake. Despite this, many people just have the same fear of snakes as they do of spiders to the point that they stamp their feet while walking through a forest. This, so I am told, will scare off the snakes before they have a chance to make themselves seen and, therefore, send them slithering off back in the direction they came from. Now, consider if you were the harmless snok in question that is being frightened by the sound of stomping boots. I'd be asking myself the question:

Look, I am harmless anyway and why do you insist on giving me a headache too?

In my ten years, I have seen approximately five long, slightly chubby, black snakes that I assumed was the harmless snok. After comparing photos of the snok against the other called the huggorm, which roughly translated means stab snake, I had to re-evaluate what I had actually seen. The snakes look fairly similar although the huggorm is supposed to be larger. It's hardly reassuring if a snok has eaten well that day and can do a really good impression of a huggorm. The best advice that I can give is leave Swedish snakes alone. If you do this, they might leave you alone.

THE COCKCHAFER

Last, but not least, I have to mention a large noisy flying beetle that you'll encounter on some islands that are situated on the west and east coasts of Sweden. The cockchafer. You can't fail to notice these beetles because they sound like low flying World War I planes. They are also large, metallic green and incredibly shortsighted. It's probably really hard to diagnose an insect as having really bad eyesight, but I am making that claim right here, right now. If I could invite one of these insects to an optician, I would certainly like my claim to be proved right because these beetles just have no idea where they are flying. As a keen photographer, I tend to focus my concentration on what I am taking a picture of, and there was one particular time when the cockchafers were out in force. Not only did one fly into my back, which felt as if someone had thrown a medium sized pebble at me, one also head-butted the fence beside me, picked up a head injury and flew around in drunken circles for a while before flying onto, or into, wherever it had decided to go.

THE VERDICT

So what do magpies, deer with attitude, the adored elk, jellyfish fights and confused insects mean to Sweden when compared to the UK? You could take it to mean that animals are more frightened in England and if you think about it, what animal wouldn't be? The proximity between them and humans in the UK is much closer than that of Sweden because the UK is one of the most densely populated countries in Europe. Does this really explain why the wildlife acts so nonchalantly?

If you think about it, Sweden hasn't been involved in any wars for well over 200 years, and society does have the reputation of being friendly and non-threatening. Maybe the wildlife has become so accustomed to this that it believes it can get away with staring you down, eating your flowers or crops right from under your nose, and stealing your freshly made sandwich out of your hand. There is no explanation for the poor confused, shortsighted Cockchafer or why the white jellyfish should anticipate being used as a makeshift snowball, but at least you should know what to expect when you see a magpie playing chicken with you.

WHAT YOU HAVE LEARNT FROM THIS CHAPTER

- Bears are just as human as we are when going to the toilet.

- Deer will eat anything.

- Magpies are tough.

- Camouflage for sandwiches is a good idea when seagulls are about.

- The back legs of an elk are targets for midnight motorists.

- Some insects need glasses.

- White jellyfish make a good snowball alternative.

2. ENTERTAINMENT

DAYTIME TV

Whenever you go on holiday, you're always likely to switch on the TV first out of curiosity to check how different it is. When I first moved to Sweden, I noticed a number of things that stood out like a streaker at Wimbledon. Daytime TV was especially cheap. The morning TV presenters, Richard and Judy, had been replaced with strange, funny phone-in quiz shows that were so ridiculously easy it was a shock when some contestants got the answer wrong. The hosts themselves were never going to become famous or move up to a well produced quiz anytime soon, and it looked as though they were being paid by the word, as they never stopped jabbering between calls. They were probably paid extra if they kept a straight face if, or more likely, when a contestant got the answer wrong. One such occasion arose while I was watching one of these shows:

"What is a language?

A. Satsuma B. Tangerine C. Mandarin D. Orange

Buzzzz! Yes. Fredrik from Örebro and the answer is...

Fredrik: Satsuma

No. I'm sorry. It's not!"

I can't imagine what pain the host went through as he stifled his laugh when the caller got that question so wrong. If I had been the TV host, I wouldn't have been able to resist mocking the contestant and might have said something like: I'm sorry, you're wrong. If you think my Swedish is bad, you should hear my Satsuma.

In between these cheap, throw away shows, came the infomercials from the USA that included the latest devices that sweated away fat, cut up cucumber in less than five seconds, and one that featured a sceptical Mr T advertising a new microwave/grill type device, speaking the immortal words:

"I pity the foo' who tries to get this down."

The infomercials that really had me stumped featured a grizzly bear that had probably been drafted in from some circus in town, or maybe that bear from Skansen, using a new type of inflatable bed. The promise that even this bed could take the weight of Gentle Ben, even after a heavy meal prepared by Mr T was all fine and well, but the makers of the bed didn't mention that the bear had had its claws clipped. I'd like to see this inflatable bed stand up to being poked and slashed by Freddy Krueger's slasher hands. Had they made this bed claw-proof too? Before I could answer any of these questions, another infomercial featuring the same bear was being broadcast to the Swedish public. After the bear had awoken from its sleep on the non-slashable inflatable bed, the bear was now being forced up a stepladder to prove that it could withstand its weight, get to the top and change a light bulb. Now, I was pretty sure that there weren't a lot of people who had a pet bear, let alone one that could walk up a stepladder and change a light bulb. So I guessed that this stepladder was being aimed at the morbidly overweight market, as they obviously needed this stepladder to illuminate their homes. Maybe the bear that I had met and annoyed at Skansen was so human-like that it needed all of these items plus the microwave/grill type thing Mr T liked.

The cheap quiz shows have all but fizzled out in Sweden but the infomercials still remain, clogging up an hour of morning TV when something better could be shown.

TV COMMERCIALS

Although infomercials from the States are awful, the reverse could be said for some of Sweden's home-grown commercials. Being both funny and quite musical, Swedish commercials actually have some humour in them, and as much as I hate to admit it, I actually prefer some of them to actual programmes. Take, for example, the adverts for the supermarket chain ICA that uses a running storyline with the same characters every time. British people could draw a direct comparison to the OXO cube adverts from the '80s and '90s, and it goes to prove that the Swedes have a similar sense of humour. There was an advert for a nasal spray featuring bogeys as soldiers that wanted to dig in and stay put in the nostrils, while another for foot fungus had toes that sang "I've had enough!". Imagination is not lost here.

When it comes to actual shows, programs, and films, Sweden goes from one extreme to another from slapstick humour to dark melancholy. Highly unfashionable, slapstick farces, called *buskis*, are shown at prime time and are something to be cringed at. A popular line of comedy films called Jönssonligan can be slotted into this category and is not so far away from slipping on a banana skin or "he's behind you" humour. Not every Swede will watch this kind of film and many prefer British or American humour instead, including classic sitcoms like Blackadder, Monty Python or Seinfeld, which is still shown to this day. There is one thing the Swedes do well and that is melancholia.

CHRISTMAS TV

T'was around Christmas time, after the dinner had been consumed and stomachs were digesting that we settled down to watch an entertaining film. After consulting the TV guide, there was a comedy about to be shown on one of the channels. Thinking that it would be a good idea, we switched over to the film that was about a family getting together at Christmas time. We thought it would be great entertainment for the afternoon, but we were quickly thrown into a world of man and wife arguments and potential divorce. Thinking this was slightly odd, I checked the guide again and it described the film as a comedy. Turning my attention back to the film, which had descended into violent fighting, I looked again at the guide and double-checked that the word comedy had not entered my brain through another subliminal method. Comedy. Even if this film had been described as a black comedy, it still wouldn't have accurately described it and it would have been the

21

blackest of comedies I had seen. If this was Sweden's idea of a comedy, I would have a hard time getting used to it.

After I had switched off the film, I was then presented with something that is only shown at Christmas time in Sweden. In the UK, 3 p.m. on Christmas Day will mean watching, or not watching, The Royal Christmas Message where the current King or Queen will address his or her loyal subjects with his or her thoughts of the year. Typically, The Royal Christmas Message won't have an impact on anything at all. Sweden does the same thing, but replaces the royalty of the UK with Donald Duck and friends instead, which will also have no impact on anything but at least does it in a fun way. In fact, they show the same cartoon every year in the way of a tradition. It's really something when Disney can have the monopoly over Christmas TV, mostly in English, in Sweden. I'm not sure how it all came about, but I think the UK should campaign for something similar to be shown instead of the Royal Christmas Message. I'm voting for Pepé Le Pew.

On New Year's Eve, *Grevinnan och Betjänten* by Lauri Wylie, known as *Dinner For One* in English, is also shown every year, as well as in Germany, Denmark and Norway, where it is particularly popular. Written and performed by Brits and filmed in Britain, it was originally aired in 1963 and features a butler looking after an elderly host, whose guests have all sadly turned up their toes. One of the most famous lines is "the same procedure as every year" and is commonly flung out there randomly by Swedes. Again, it is strange being a Brit and watching something British in Sweden that has been quite obviously ignored by its home country. *Dinner For One* certainly never caught on in Britain and you'd have trouble finding anyone knowing any quotes from it.

THE CENSORS

Putting the shock of Donald Duck and *Dinner For One* behind me, I was yet again, open-mouthed by something quite different. Sweden does not have any rules against using swearwords at any time of the day and my shock was highlighted when one film character said the word f*ck. Don't get me wrong. I'm not prude and swearwords don't bother me as long as they are used appropriately but this word ambushed me at 3 p.m.. Swedes generally have the rule that English swearwords don't have any meaning and can therefore be used whenever, wherever. One commercial for a beer used the phrase "you utter ba*tard" which amused some British friends that were visiting. Using swearwords, especially English ones, just seemed to be ok wherever you turn. Although the rules have changed in the UK, there used to be something called the watershed where films with swearwords shown before 9 p.m. were dubbed by unsuitable voices and childish words. The aim of this process was to eliminate the chance of any young children, who might have been watching, going out into the street and repeating what Clint Eastwood just said, for example. Instead, the censors unwittingly turned what were originally intended as serious hard-edged films into comedy films. As I mentioned Clint Eastwood earlier, it's only fair that I mention *Heartbreak Ridge*, a gritty army film about drill sergeants and tough soldiers:

Original line: "…big leatherneck, jarhead m??*f?**er!"

Censored: "…big leatherneck, jarhead maggot farmer!"

What made this even worse was the fact that the voice that dubbed over the swearwords was totally different from the actors. Sometimes, the dubbed swearwords made it sound as if the actors voice had just broken and puberty was just around the corner again.

Another example of when censored movies attack is the unfortunate *Robocop* that had the censors working overtime to convert a gory, violent film into the funniest of comedies:

Original line: "Once I even called the boss "asshole!"

Censored: "Once I even called the boss "airhead!"

What an insult! I bet the boss was so riled that he grabbed a gun and sprayed the insulting crook with water, after he had thrown a cushion at him beforehand.

Whilst on the subject of films, I can't go without mentioning the Oscars. We all know that sleek golden statue of a knight standing on a reel of film. It's the ultimate prize of the film industry. Of course, every country has its own individual film award. The UK has the BAFTA award, a sleek theatrical mask that has become an internationally recognised symbol. Sweden has…, well, a not so sleek looking beetle called a Guldbagge (Golden Beetle) as its official film award. It's not even gold. It's made out of copper and is enameled and gilded with the winner's name stuck on the underside of the beetle. I have no explanation to why it's not as sleek as its British and American counterparts, but I do have an explanation to as why they chose a beetle. The designer of the award likened the shimmer of a flying gold beetle to that of a filmstrip moving through a projector. That's what I call a vivid imagination!

MUSIC SHOWS

Moving on from badly dubbed films, another curious game show popped up that made me question
how much Swedes loved music. I was horrified when
I saw a show called *Så Ska Det Låta*, which translated
means *that's more like it*. I will explain the concept of
the show before I go ahead and insult it first. Two
teams of three celebrities, with team captains seated
at pianos, solve music clues and questions by singing
the answers in the form of well-known songs. The
celebrities who take part aren't always from the music world and that becomes apparent after listening
to them butcher a classic that you might love. The
celebrities will go to such extreme lengths in singing
the answer, that they will sing almost a whole song,
in front of a studio audience, in front of the viewers
at home, with complete disregard for the fact that
they might actually be tone deaf. The show is an hour
long, and is responsible for me making more cups of
tea than I can possibly drink, making sure I stay in
the toilet longer than I need, probably after all the
tea, and looking for any possible distraction to stop
my ears from bleeding. The only example of this
show in the UK is *Never Mind The Buzzcocks* where
celebs have to hum a tune for the others to guess
what it is. It sounds similar, but the sarcastic nature
of Never Mind The Buzzcocks, and the fact that the
team captains are comedians, means that nothing is

taken seriously at all. When compared to *Så Ska Det Låta*, there is a certain amount of semi-seriousness about it, as light hearted as it tries to be. It's certainly not for the musically squeamish.

THE EUROVISION SONG CONTEST

The Swedes are crazy about the Eurovision Song Contest. When this competition swings by in the UK, most people will usually grumble and say to themselves that it's a pile of rubbish and that they won't be watching, knowing damn well that they will anyway. Once someone in the UK has watched it and the winner, or winners, have been sprayed with confetti and bombarded with camera flashes, they'll still usually say that it was a load of rubbish and won't be watching it next year.

The UK song is usually just announced to the general public without any consultation about what it is and who is performing it. This goes some way to explaining why some of the more recent song entries from the UK have been pretty sub-standard. Take into consideration that Javine, Daz Sampson, and Scooch were all entered over three consecutive years of crud, just to hammer home how much we didn't care. Compare this, if you will, to what the Swedish public go through. They get to see the heats in various cities, they get to vote on those songs with two songs from each heat going through to the final and two going through to a second chance round. This part of the Eurovision is called Melodifestivalen.

The second chance round can be roughly translated as the 'songs that weren't really that well liked the first time' round. It's almost torture having to sit through the songs that didn't win or come second in any of the heats but it wastes an hour of TV time, and you have to remember, all the money raised by the telephone voting goes to charity. This is a good thing for the charities, but it won't spare your ears! Sweden then votes for their favourite song in the final which means, yet again, you'll have to listen to the songs again just like the second chance round. By the time the final comes around, you'll have heard all of the songs on TV, on the radio, on someone's mobile phone on the tube or just rattling around in your brain from the umpteen times you have already heard it. It's a far cry from the UK where the public are just presented with a song and just told: This is it. Bite me if you don't like it.

The actual Eurovision Song Contest is taken seriously by most in Sweden with arguments arising as to who likes what song the most and why. I have been to many a Eurovision Song Contest gathering where people almost analyse the songs that are being presented to them. The usual "crap" and "like that one" that I would say if in the UK, doesn't cut the mustard here and Sweden seems to require you to have a really good reason to why you like a certain song. Even if the Swedish entry is really bad, people always want it to do well and when it doesn't, newspapers label it as a fiasco. The UK audience, however, are fickle. Bearing in mind that the general UK audience say that they don't take the Eurovision seriously, it doesn't stop them from commenting on their song coming last or almost last. If this happens, there are usually hails of protest saying that the rest of Europe must really hate us for political reasons and that's the reason they didn't vote for us. The British don't even take into consideration that they may have entered a really duff song, and it may deserve its placing. If a song does well, you'll never hear anyone complain. As I said—fickle.

THEATRES AND THEME PARKS

Entertainment is not just restricted to TV, film and song contests. Numerous theatres and stages largely support the thespian world all across Sweden. This is a good thing when you want to avoid sing-a-long TV quizzes.

One of the advantages of living in one the cities in Sweden is that you can go to the theme parks, open from April to December, whenever you want when you buy a yearly pass. The obvious drawback to this is that this only covers the entrance fee and, once you are in, you'll have to fork out to go on any of the rides. This isn't as bad as it sounds because if there is a band playing, magic show, theatrical performance or Xmas market advertised, you can get past the gatekeepers and visit. When you consider that the rock giants, Alice Cooper and Bryan Adams have played on Gröna Lund's stage in Stockholm, parting with some kronor for a yearly pass is a good bargain.

One thing that sets Swedish theme parks apart from the UK is their location. They are situated in city centres, making it easy for everybody to access. Liseberg, the theme park in Gothenburg, is situated right in the centre beside busy crossroads. You might imagine that a theme park in the middle of a city would be too noisy, but it's actually hard to hear any noise at all. Several theme parks in the UK have had noise restrictions applied to them to dampen the noise they make, even though they are situated away from housing developments. I'm not sure how Liseberg or Gröna Lund have managed to dampen their noise pollution, but I can say that they have done it without erecting walls lined with egg cartons.

Liseberg left a lasting impression on me when I visited the Christmas market for the first time. No tree had been left untouched from light bulbs. None of the Liseberg green bunny mascots had been spared a Christmas hat. No visitor had been spared the minus temperatures that Sweden was experiencing at the time of year. Liseberg also had an ice bar.

A small bar made of…you guessed it…ice. A slightly strange concept bearing in mind the season was winter and the whole of Gothenburg was almost one big ice cube. The ice bar enticed people in to experience sub-arctic temperatures, encased in ice. Being a glutton for punishment, I paid my entrance fee, along with my girlfriend, and were given Eskimo costumes and a vodka drink ticket each. I wondered if asking for my drink on the rocks would be seen as an insult so I decided not to risk it, instead finding out that my glass would be the rock and made out of ice. Sipping on our freezing cold vodkas, on frozen sculpted designer furniture, there was one thing that struck us. This really was the epitome of cold and the outside temperature had actually just been a preliminary test. After we had sipped down our vodkas in less time than it takes to realise how cold it was, we walked outside and realised that it now actually felt warm. Now the ice bar made sense. Sweden can get cold but spare a thought for Eskimos and penguins.

Not everyone will like theme parks that feature scary rides. Some will want to just wander about, choosing a go on the dodgem cars instead. The dodgems might be less of a heart attack risk than a go on a roller-coaster, but there is something even more scarier that afflicts theme parks—the mascot. Liseberg is a good example because they have opted for a buck-toothed, lime green, bunny with a spotty tie as their mascot. To inflict some form of painful entertainment, Liseberg employs people to dress up in bunny mascot costumes to meet, greet, and generally scare customers. It has been said that the poor Liseberg bunny looks evil, and it's not hard to understand why. With huge ears, big glaring black eyes, a red nose and standing at a height that dwarfs taller children, it's easy to see why kids, and maybe some adults, might be experiencing bunny nightmares after a Liseberg visit.

One of the other main attractions is the lottery wheel where you can win a huge bar of chocolate or a bag of crisps. And when I say huge, I mean huge as in gigantic. As luck would have it, there is a chocolate bar called Plopp, which has a wheel dedicated to it. Not one to shy away from the wheel of Plopp, there was one time when I put a few kronor down on all of the numbers except one. The girl started the wheel, and I nervously watched the Plopp wheel spin. I glanced at my prize. A huge Plopp was waiting for me if everything went well. As the wheel came to a stop, it landed on the number that I hadn't put any kronor on. This was typical!

"Ah crap!" I said looking at the girl in a pleading 'let me have a Plopp way', "The only number I didn't bet on and now I am Ploppless!"

I wasn't sure if the girl was really up for any Plopp jokes as she had heard them all before from other English people who might have given the wheel of Plopp a spin just for its namesake. She asked if I wanted another go and I decided that a big Plopp was probably out of reach for me. As I walked away, I saw a kid stumble past, struggling to carry one of the huge Plopp bars that I had tried to win. Although I had lost in my attempt to win one, I was generally entertained by a large chocolate bar that seemed to be swallowing a small child. Was there just one huge Plopp inside it or lots of little Plopps? Did the kid actually like Plopp? Did the kid know that whichever way you looked at it, he had a lot of Plopp to eat? Even though revenge might have taken the form of tooth decay, I still to this day, am jealous of anyone who has been lucky to experience a big Plopp at Liseberg.

THINGS YOU HAVE LEARNT FROM THIS CHAPTER

- Bears hibernate on inflatable beds.

- Bears can change light bulbs using a ladder.

- Swear as much as you want when using English swearwords.

- Maggot farms must exist, as there are maggot farmers.

- Being tone deaf isn't the end of your career.

- Having nightmares about scary green bunnies could happen.

- You have to take the Eurovision Song Contest seriously.

- Donald Duck is the king of Sweden.

- Satsuma is a language.

- There's nothing like a big Plopp.

3. LANGUAGE

FIRST IMPRESSIONS

When I moved in 2003, I didn't have any opinion of the Swedish language other than what the Swedish chef said and that wasn't much. If I used him as an example, the Swedish language would be about singing a song in gibberish whilst throwing chickens around at the same time.

The first bump that brought me down to earth was my very first visit to Gothenburg. It was a cold November day with some melting snow on the ground as the plane landed at Gothenburg City airport. There was nothing that really stuck out about the Swedish language at this point, until I jumped off the bus in the middle of the city.

As I looked around, I noticed that the Central Station in Gothenburg was actually called Centralstation. Brilliant. The language was going to be a doddle if this was called the same thing here, I thought to myself. Unfortunately, this illusion was shattered when this stop was read out over a loud speaker by the tram announcers:

"Nesta: Centrraal Sta-hoo-nan."

What? What did he say? Sta-hoo-what? The large sign said Central Station not what he just said! I had to swallow my heart back into its rightful place again as I had to comprehend what had just happened.

As I began to walk through part of Gothenburg, I saw signs in shop windows that read slut and really hoped that meant something different to what it meant in English. Other such signs also raised a wry smile as I passed them by including farthinder, infart and then utfart. It certainly was a lot of farts and I wondered what they all meant as I carried on up the street to my final destination.

As I passed bus and tram stops, I started to feel very scared of the Swedish language. I passed one stop called Hagakyrkan, which made me stop and take notes. How would I go about pronouncing that after Central Station had disappointed me so much? Hagga-cry-kan? Hajjy-crew-khan? The name of the stop I had to get to was called Allhelgonakyrkan and it was at this point that I raised my hands to the sky, shrugged my shoulders and decided that I would wait to learn the language before I tried to pronounce my home's own tram stop, All-goony-cry-khan. It could have been a dinosaur for all I knew.

LEARNING THE LANGUAGE

In 2004, I enrolled in my first Swedish language course, SFI, which stands for Svenska för invandrare (Swedish for immigrants). Of course, not knowing what that actually meant, I assumed that invandrare meant invader or something similar. The course itself was 4 days a week with Wednesdays off for good behaviour. It was strange to go back to education again after 10 years of being away from it. As I didn't have a job, and had plans to live in Sweden indefinitely, I would need the language, and if this course was good enough to teach me how to pronounce my tram stop, it was good enough for me!

Getting off at another stop that I couldn't pronounce, I made my way to the college, found my room and took a seat. Three nervous looking class mates nodded their hellos at me and I did the same back. You could have cut the air with a hacksaw. Although I already knew some words from listening to music and from TV, I still felt very unprepared for any lesson. The teacher entered the room, faster than a whirlwind and with much gusto. Talking loudly to herself as she made her way to her desk, she clapped loudly and started speaking to us as if we knew some Swedish already. Nobody could understand anything she said and we all looked at each other for some kind of support and backup plan. This was not a good start. We might have assumed that she was telling us to be quiet, as this is what most teachers say at the start of a lesson, but she could have been saying anything, like: I am the anti-Christ of Swedish language courses and I will roast one of you over a spit as a sacrifice to my god. We all stayed very quiet.

"Jag he-et-er Ann-a. Jag he-et-er Ann-aaa," she said as she rose from her seat and wrote exactly the same thing on the whiteboard. "Ja-ag het-teeer An-naaaaa!"

Yes. We all understood this basic phrase from our guidebooks. Her name was Anna. We got that. It was going to be a long week. As she said this phrase one more time whilst sitting down, I noticed a sign above the door that read:

Ursäkta mig att jag har kommit för sent.

Translated this meant:

I'm sorry that I am late.

This had me worried. Surely that was some kind of joke or something that had been left there since the '50s along with a cane for a beating if you dared to show up late.

My hopes were dashed when another Englishman entered the room five minutes late. The teacher coughed and got his attention. Confused, he turned around and looked at the teacher.

"Du måste läsa det!" said the teacher (you must read that!).

"What?" replied the confused Englishman.

""What" är inte svenska. Inte svenska. Du måste läsa det!" she said, pointing with a stick ("what" is not Swedish. Not Swedish. You must read that!).

"I think she wants you read that sign, mate," I said, getting a stern look from the mistress of Swedish.

"Svenska. Du måste prata svenska!" (Swedish. You must talk Swedish!).

Of course, I would have gladly talked Swedish to her. I just needed to learn it first, which was why I was there.

"Err sackta meeg att jag har comet for sent," said the Englishman.

It wasn't a half bad attempt.

"Du kan sitta nu," said the teacher (you can sit now).

This had me worried already and we were only five minutes into the lesson. I felt as if this was some kind of cruel experiment where old teaching methods were used as some kind of torture. I was stuck in a course that felt as if it had been designed for primary school children where I would be punished for turning up late. In fact, turning up late was the cardinal sin for which students were thrown off the course. Students, who had missed weeks, seemed to get away with it. I put it down to Swedish efficiency and anal time keeping and left it at that.

I had already started to encounter difficulties in the Swedish language before these lessons had begun. On a bathroom visit, I noticed a tube labelled fuktcreme that jump-started my brain into thinking what kind of cream it could be. Was it cream that didn't work or do anything? Surely not.

The main mission of my first lesson came when I was given the task of finding the Swedish word for snail. I had learnt the word for slug, which was snigel, but I couldn't find the word for snail no matter how hard I looked. I eventually gave up on my quest to find it and wrote down snigel med hus (slug with house) on my answer sheet and hoped for the best. The teacher, showing some human emotion of laughing, corrected me and revealed that the Swedes use snigel to describe both slug and snail. It was like killing two mollusks with one stone.

During my Swedish studies, different language learning techniques were introduced to me, techniques that I hadn't come across at any other time on my way from a child to an adult. Techniques that were quite frankly bizarre to me and I would probably dismiss as soon as I got home. One of these techniques was learning through bongos. To really grasp the rhythm of the language, the teacher used a tape that tapped out the rhythm of words for us to follow. So, for "Hej! Hur är det?" there would be four bongo beats. Most of the class tried to conceal their laughter by putting their hand over their mouths, whilst others just simply looked bemused by the whole experience. The teacher, upon seeing our amusement, looked quite peeved but didn't say anything. Thump-bong-crash! I thought to myself as I tried to think what - this is crap - would sound like through bongos.

Another technique made students use their arms like propellers when trying to understand the rhythm of the language. We rotated our arms with a pointed finger round in a circle and said a word at the same time. It was rather like trying to pat your head and rub your stomach in some ways. Both were completely pointless. Yes, I understood that the Swedish language had rhythm, but there had to be a better way to describe it. For example, this method worked ok with small words like polis, but once you moved onto compound words, the system collapsed. I almost felt like asking the teacher: Try saying Föreningssparbanken and wave your finger round in a circle.

The third and final technique that was bounced off our brains featured a red sock that represented somebody's tongue. By shaping his hand, the teacher tried to tell us that this is what a tongue should do when trying to pronounce specific words. If the class had had knowledge of phonetics then this teacher would have had it made, but it failed because most students could only see *South Park*'s Mr Garrison in front of them. If I had tried to use all of these techniques together to learn Swedish, I would have probably ended up looking like a contortionist who had just sucked a lemon.

After scraping through the course with a pass, I started to get a little bit of confidence in speaking the language, although I still had problems with understanding the person on the street. It would take more than bongos, waving my arms around, and a tough teacher to get me to a decent level. This is why the Swedish language course doesn't end with just the basics. There used to be three additional courses called SASG, SASA, and SASB, that are now called Swedish 5, 6 and 7, that all take roughly 6 months each. Bearing this in mind, you are looking at 2 years of studying if you do them all consecutively and this is a fair chunk of time unless you look at doing them in the evenings. However, after passing SFI, I did at least find out that invandrare meant immigrant and not invader.

TELLING THE TIME

You might be slightly prepared to go out into the Swedish world armed with just SFI, but nothing quite prepares you for simple things you take for granted. Telling the time, for example, is one of these simple things. You'll have to learn how to tell the time and start from scratch again. Yes. It's true. The cunning

Swedes have a different way of saying the time and my head felt as if it were going to explode if someone asked me what the time was. Here is what you must know before you reveal the time to someone in Sweden:

Hur mycket är klockan? – What is the time?

This sounds relatively simple but if you have the mindset to translate directly into English, the Swedish becomes - How much is the clock?, to which you could reply:

About 20 quid I think!

Klockan är halv 8 – The time is half past 7.

Yes. This is true too. The Swedes work on the principle of is the glass half empty or half full. In the case of a half past the hour query, the clock reads 30 minutes to the next hour. So in this example, it is 30 minutes to 8 o' clock instead of 30 minutes past 7. Got it? Don't relax just yet!

The next art of Swedish time keeping is the 25

past and 25 minutes to times.

Klockan är 5 i halv 8 and klockan är 5 över halv 8.

Translated directly means:

It's five to half past 7 or it's five over half past 7.

Confused? You should be. I know I was. The Swedes read the 25 to and past times as 5 minutes to the half past the hour. Combine this with their pint half full, half empty method and you'll be scratching your head for a long time. There has been many a time when I have turned up an hour early or late for something when it comes to these times...ok so it's 5 minutes over the half past so that means it is something:35. Yep. That's right now, half 8 means 8.30...yes, that's right, no hold on. Maybe not. Five minutes over the half... what? So if you are having a complete conversation with someone, it can quickly become really confusing, when you first start living in Sweden.

"Hur mycket är klockan?"

"I don't remember actually, it was a Christmas

present from my parents. I reckon it must be worth 30 pounds at least."

"Nej. Vad är klockan?"

"What is the clock? I think it is a Citizen model. It's certainly not a Rolex."

"Nej. Du förstår inte. Är klockan 13 eller 14 eller någonting?"

"Ah ha! You want to know what the time is? Why didn't you say so? Just to impress you, I'll try replying in Swedish."

"Varsågod." (go ahead.)

(looks at watch and it reads 13:35)

"Ok. Erm. Klockan är 5 i halv 1. Nej. Klockan är 5 över 1. Nej. 35 över halv i 2. Nej. Herregud."

"Är klockan 5 över halv 2?"

"Nej. I'll get this. In a minute. Give me a chance. 5 över 35 över nästan 1 men kanske 2? Oh sod it! It's one thirty-five, ok?"

"Tack!"

52 WEEKS

Although not strictly a language issue, you do have to keep your wits about you when someone is talking about times. Another thing Swedes do is to refer to weeks in the year with numbers. The first week of

January is called vecka 1, then vecka 2, and so on and so on. That's not so hard to understand except when somebody starts talking about going on holiday.

- I'm taking week 34 and 35 off.

Leaving the typical non Swede asking:

- And when is that exactly?

It's very hard to figure out what time of year it is when it is referred to as a week number. I have learnt week 1 and week 52 but apart from that, everything else is in the middle is a little hazy.

- We can do that week 23.

If Swedes are going to start referring to weeks in number terms then maybe they should start doing that with the days too.

- Yeah ok. I'll be doing this on day 265 and doing this day 132. Work that one out clever clogs!

Many Swedes will carry diaries with them that list all the week numbers as well as name days too. You see, every day also has a name given to it, and if you happen to share the same name with a day, you might get a cake as a present. If the Swedes have to carry diaries with them to figure out what week is what, then it goes to prove that this system must be fairly hard to master.

JUST SAY YES

The biggest pitfall in the Swedish language is that there are many ways of saying the word yes. As you can imagine, this can make things fairly difficult if you don't know what could potentially mean yes.

Words in Swedish that mean yes are as follows:

Ah.

Mmm.

Ja.

Nja.

Jo.

? and ?

As you can imagine, the above list can trick out the most observant of people, and if you are wondering what the question marks are for, then let me explain them. There are two ways of saying yes with noises. Imagine sipping on an imaginary tea and missing the rim of the cup completely. This kind of toothless, sucking sound, can mean yes. The other question mark is for another noise that is basically yep whilst taking a deep breath at the same time. It sounds as if someone is having a hard time breathing and having a quick asthma attack. This can mean yes as well.

To highlight the problem of saying yes in Swedish, take into consideration a story about a friend of mine.

After moving from the USA, my friend settled in Sweden and had learnt the language a little bit. During a conversation, she was asked if she wanted to be a teacher for an evening class. She gave the question a - hmmm - and thought nothing more of it. A - hmmm - in the UK or USA usually means that you are thinking something over or pondering a question. It certainly does not mean yes.

A week later, she was called by the college who wanted to finalise the details of her class.

"So, you start at 19:00 and the lesson lasts for 2 hours and…"

"Hold on, woah, woah. I didn't say yes to being the teacher!"

"But you said 'mmm'."

"Yes, but that meant I was thinking about it and not 'mmm' as in yes"

"Oh.."

My friend did eventually have to take the evening class just because she mumbled - hmmm. So as you can see from this unlucky example, knowing what means yes can be very important.

SWEARING IN SWEDISH

The question people ask me the most, especially the British, is about swearing in Swedish. The first thing I looked up were swearwords, not because I am the type that would use them, but to be able to tell whether or not somebody was annoyed with me.

Swearing in Swedish is a tricky thing because that also has a system that you have to remember. As if it wasn't hard enough already to remember what the time is and how to say yes. Most of the swearwords relate to the devil and hell with some not really relating to anything, which makes them sound funny when used. It's probably not what the Swedes had in mind with their swearwords, but when you come from a nation that's not particularly angry at anything, you can understand why they use some of them.

The world *jävla* in its true sense just means devil but can also mean damn if you are just talking nicely and not in anger. If you are angry and slip in the word *jävla*, it is then transformed into f**k. So how do you know when someone is actually angry with you or just mucking around? It's a good question, but you just have to read someone's tone of voice and hope for the best. If you have mistakenly made a noise and said yes to something when you didn't

49

mean to, then it's a good bet that the *jävla* would mean f**k, not damn and certainly not devil. It does make it hard when you have to swear at someone and call them a devil at the same time.

Just to confuse things even further, there are swearwords that don't actually seem to be that insulting. Take, for example, the word *skitstövel* which means b**tard but translated means shit boot. It doesn't exactly sound threatening to call someone this when you come from another country because there's always that thing in the back of your mind that says you have just called someone a shit boot.

On the flip side of the coin, there are words and phrases in Swedish that sound like swearwords but actually aren't. *Skitsnack* means bullshit but is not especially rude in Swedish terms to say. *Skit samma* means never mind but uses the word *skit*, which is shit literally translated. When *skit samma* was used by my girlfriend's mother, I looked at her with my mouth open, thinking that she had just sworn but as it turned out, she had not.

Now put all the above in the context of an angry, misunderstood conversation and you might get:

- Är klockan 13:35? (Is the time 13:35?)

- I still don't know. I can't tell the time in Swedish yet.

- Skit samma. (Never mind)

- What did you call me?

- Ingenting. (Nothing)

- Yes you did. You called me shithead or something.

- Nej. Det gjorde jag inte. Pucko! (No. I didn't. Idiot!)

- Did you just call me a devil? Or was that damn? Or something worse?

- Skit samma. (Never mind)

- There you go again. What is your problem buddy? Why do you hate me so much?

- Herregud! Du pratar skitsnack. Jag hatar inte dig. (Oh my god! You are talking bullshit. I don't hate you.)

- Right. That's the last time you insult me. You're off my Christmas card list.

- Fan. (Damn!)

Not many people get angry with me so it's not a problem, but when I hear an angry conversation with swearwords, I just laugh, as it really does not sound like someone being angry. If I happen to get into an angry exchange with a Swede, it'll be more likely that I have just laughed my head off at them swearing at me than for a legitimate reason.

USING YOUR SWEDISH IN THE OUTSIDE WORLD

Once you have learnt all of the above and mastered verbs and grammar, you can attempt to speak it out in Swedish public. I was under the impression that once I had learnt Swedish, I could then go to Denmark or Norway and be able to speak to them too. It doesn't work like that. Danish, although related, sounds much different when spoken and is often referred to as speaking with a potato down the back of the throat. Norwegian, on the other hand, is closer to Swedish, although they tend to speak with more rhythm and melody than the Swedes do. However, this doesn't mean you can go to Norway and try to speak Swedish because even though they will understand you, there are some little differences that I found out at my expense.

On a trip to Norway, we arrived in central Oslo and got stopped by a random customs check. It was a harmless visit and I was determined to speak Swedish. There shouldn't have been a problem, and I wanted to show off what several months had actually taught me. The customs officer started to ask us questions with squinted eyes and bleeping electrical gadgets armed and ready. When asked why we were in Oslo, I confidently replied:

"Dopfest."

This would have been completely harmless had I been in Sweden but this was Norway and we were faced with a very serious customs officer. *Dop* means christening in Swedish and fest means party. That was the reason why we were there that weekend. As the word left my tongue, I felt smug with myself that I knew the answer to his question, and I smiled at him slightly, pleased that I had got this one right. Unfortunately for me, *dopfest* means drugs party in Norwegian, leaving my girlfriend in a panic, waving her hands at the customs officer saying: "dåpfest… dåpfest" which is the Norwegian word for *dopfest*. It was only one letter out, and a slight phonetic difference, but it didn't matter. I'd put my foot in it, and the squinty officer looked as if his eyes were about to heal up when we tried to explain that it was a christening, not a drugs party. When he let us go, I looked over my shoulder where I saw him talking into his walky-talky, squinting at me, still not believing that we were there for a very innocent reason.

DIALECTS

If you believe you'll be sitting pretty after having learnt the Swedish language to a good level, think again! Dialects can hamper your progress in your proficiency of the Swedish language. If you come from the UK, then you'll know Scouse and Geordie can be hard to understand. In Birmingham, they use words like *mardy* and *bostin* that aren't used anywhere else in the country. Every region of Sweden has their dialect and will therefore have their own way of saying things. If you live or come from Skåne, in the south of Sweden, you are usually the prime target for dialect mimicking, mainly because it's a cross between Swedish and Danish. Remember how I mentioned the hot potato down the back of the throat? The Skåne accent is not a million miles away from that and, sometimes, the accent can be so thick that the rest of the Swedish population need subtitles when a show is set there. A direct comparison would be with Newcastle or Scotland where some southern Brits will not understand them either. For example, when I was a young lad, and on work experience for a furniture chain, I got a phone call from a Scottish customer who I couldn't understand. I didn't want to sound like an idiot so I just kept saying yes to anything he said. It turned out that he was no ordinary Scottish customer. It was an angry Scottish customer; an angry Scottish customer who had not had his furniture delivered on time, and when it had arrived, it wasn't what he ordered. Saying yes to everything he said turned out not to be a good idea when I had agreed to pay him compensation and deliver his furniture the following week. I imagined that the angry Scottish customer probably busted out of his shirt, with shirt buttons flying, his skin turning a shade of pea green, roaring whilst beating his tartan chest to become the incredible Scot, ready to pick up a sofa and throw it at me.

When I have a conversation with someone from Skåne, I tackle it in the same way as I do with Geordie or Scottish. I usually look at them with a question mark on my face to signal that I have no idea what they are saying.

Gothenburgers are well known for their more jokey accent, incorporating a kind of melody that nobody else has. Stockholmers will stand from their 500km distance and laugh at them for it, but Stockholmers aren't devoid of having the finger of ridicule pointed at them either. The Stockholm accent is seen as a neutral upper class accent that only the successful bourgeois speak. The first time I encountered the Stockholmer accent was on a train where the announcer started every sentence with "Njaaaaa" which is something that only some Stockholmers do, or so I am told. If a Stockholmer is one of the typically successful bourgeois that has the slicked back hair and hangs out at Stureplan of a Friday evening, then you might hear them use the words *najs*, which means nice, and the expression soft soft, which also means nice but in a more poncy way.

The further north you travel in Sweden, the slower the dialect gets with people in Norrland having a knack of drawing out words longer than they should be. For example, someone from Norrland or a Finnish Swede will say:

- Pååå andra siiiiidan vääääägen (on the other side of the road)

The emphasis here is on most of the vowels in the same way a Northamptonian will say:

- Yeaaaaaaah. Iiii've beeen there too, me duck* (Ja! Jag har varit där också min anka)

* I'm not sure why Northamptonians, especially born and bred Northamptonians, say "me duck" on the end of a sentence. Sometimes, I have heard them say "me cock" which I can't explain away either.

In Sweden, there is something called *gnällbältet*, the complaining belt, which is a phenomenon in the Swedish language. Considered to stretch from Laxå to Eskilstuna, it's the part of the country where people are supposed to talk as if they are complaining all the time. Although allegedly dying out, I have heard one person talk with the *gnällbältet* accent and it's something to behold. It's almost hard to listen to as you just want to say to that person:

- Look. Life's not that bad. Stop your bloody whining and get on with it.

They could have been talking about treating you to that holiday that you've always dreamed of for your 50th birthday present, and giving you a million kronor of spending money, but it will still sound as if they are complaining about it while they say it. Can you imagine how difficult it is for them to actually really complain? Does their dialect change from whining to normal when they do want to complain about something? There isn't anything similar in the UK to compare this to, but Australians do have the nickname of whinging poms for the Brits who do have a tendency to complain.

SWENGLISH

A phenomenon that happens to English folk who have the task of trying to speak Swedish is something called swenglish, a cross between English and Swedish. This is when a native English speaker will translate a phrase in their head from English to Swedish and then regurgitate it and hope for the best. For example, if you wanted to say: My feet got soaked on my way to work this morning, and didn't know the language so well, you might be tempted to try: Jag fått blöt fötter på min väg till arbete.. erm.. this morning. Fått does indeed mean - got - but you can't use it in this sense. Instead, you would have say: Jag blev blöt om fötterna på vägen in till jobbet imorse, which literally translated means, I became wet around the feet on the way into the job this morning. You see how difficult it is?

There are other times where you could go wrong. Many, if not all, elevators will have a chunky silver button with the word - hit - on it. When I stayed at a hotel, a troop of English tourists were also checking in at the same time. When they noticed the word - hit - on the elevator button, they commented:

"Well, these Swedes are certainly direct aren't they Brian? It says hit on this button."

The word - hit - in Swedish doesn't mean that you should hit the button with all of your force. Hit means - here - and is pronounced - heet. While I am discussing elevators, the button labelled - ned - is not the name of the guy who will rescue you if the lift suddenly breaks down. This means down. Swedes have, however, made up easy by keeping it largely the same with - upp. Fire extinguishers have the word - skum - written on them, which conjures up an image of some horrible substance being squirted out of them. I can put your mind at rest and say that this only means foam.

There are other words that native English speakers will be confused about and you will find them all in the appendix in the back of the book.

THINGS YOU HAVE LEARNT FROM THIS CHAPTER

• Irate Scottish sofa buyers can act like bears when misunderstood.

• Tram stops sound like dinosaur names.

- Learning Swedish through bongos does not work.

- Learning Swedish through semaphore also does not work.

- Learning Swedish from a teacher with a red sock on their hand relies on phonetic knowledge and, overall, does not work.

- You will have to learn to tell the time again. When the big hand is on…

- Hur mycket är klockan? doesn't mean someone wants to buy your watch.

- Turning up an hour late or an hour early can happen when your event starts at 5 over the half past to the almost o' clock.

- You won't know what time of year it is when Swedes start talking in week numbers.

- It's easy to say yes to something even when you didn't want to.

- Swedish swearwords sound funny.

- Swedish words that sound like swearwords are funny.

- Don't try to be clever with a squinty Norwegian customs officer.

- Swedish is so hard that people speaking Skånska need subtitles.

- Remember that words that look English in Swedish mean something else.

4. EDUCATION

Well known to many all around the world, Sweden has maintained the stance that education should be available to all and mostly free. It was something that I wasn't aware of before moving.

FREE EDUCATION

My first brush with education was right at the start of my tenure when I applied for SFI (Svenska för invandrare), which was completely free. In fact, all the courses after this basic course were free. When I looked more closely at other available courses, they were all free too. There seemed to be something they all had in common. Free. Of course, these were courses for adults, more commonly known as kom-vux in Sweden and could also be taken part-time in the evenings too. Yes. Sweden had this education game all figured out for the likes of me but what about homegrown, organic Swedes who have been through the system?

MY UK EDUCATION vs. SWEDISH EDUCATION

The Swedish school system starts at grundskola when children are 7 years old and finish when they are 16. After this, 3 years at gymnasiet is deeply encouraged, as finding a job with just grundskola education is difficult. Universitiet comes after gymnasiet and students can study there for years in the same way students can in the UK. The real difference is starting school at seven years old compared to my low starting age of five. I could have started lower school at the age of four as some in my class had done, but my parents chose to bypass that option. If I had started aged four, that's a whole three years difference compared to a Swede. Is there any way of gauging if the two years advance in my school start had given me any advantage over a Swede of the same age? There's no real answer to that question but you also have to take into account that *dagis* (nursery) exists from the age of one, if need be.

You'll often hear parents biting their nails in fear of not getting a dagis place for their bundle(s) of joy, and rising waiting lists for children being admitted to them can be long. Once a child has been admitted, the question still remains whether they will appreciate it or not. If my nursery experience is anything to go by, I spent most of my time trying to run away from it, longing for home. I'm not sure what I was running away from, but not even the lure of finger biscuits and a glass of milk at 3 p.m. could sway me to staying. After Thatcher was elected in 1979, the finger biscuits got the chop and the glass of milk stayed in the fridge, which gained her the rightly deserved title of "Thatcher the milk snatcher". I always wondered why we had to have finger biscuits and milk at 3 p.m. anyway. It transpired that it was a national ritual and wasn't just confined to my nursery.

It makes me wonder if Swedish children got something similar to the oddly shaped finger biscuit. If they did, I would imagine that Swedes would be efficient in their 3 p.m. snack giving abilities (maybe a free course exists for that too), giving kids a banana kaviar covered egg to be washed down with a watered down black coffee. This would prepare them to keep the same diet for when they grow into adulthood, minus the banana kaviar of course. In fact, I can't even imagine children entertaining the notion of eating that concoction of mismatched ingredients (read the food chapter!).

STUDENT LOANS & GRANTS

Although tuition costs are non-existent at university, living costs, however, aren't, and that is the same in most countries. Sweden has something called CSN which stands for Centrala studie... studiestöd... erm..., excuse me while I pop my teeth in, *Studiestödsnämnden*, who are basically the nice people who handle student loans, that are paid back when someone starts working. The student loan has a limit but is usually enough to see a student through a good number of studying years. The CSN also handles grants and a student gets a certain amount a month. A student in the UK can face hefty student loans to cover tuition costs, although there is a maintenance grant that can be claimed.

Before somebody even gets to the CSN stage, what are compulsory school days actually like in Sweden? It's difficult for me to know entirely what Swedish schoolchildren go through on their route to further education and then the job market, but here are a few things that I have noticed.

A TICK MEANS WRONG

After I had experienced going back to studies again in 2004, and throughout my time in Sweden, I had to understand the way in which teachers worked. Learning through bongos and waving-arms-in-a-circle-techniques may have been radical and probably unusual, but there was a way in which teachers did everything uniformly and that was the way they marked homework. Instead of using ticks to mean correct and crosses to mean wrong, the Swedes use R for right and a tick for wrong. This made for some confusion when I got my first verb test back from the teacher with a lot of ticks. There I was, happy that I had got almost everything right to only find out that the dunce's cap was being altered at the tailors to fit my head.

EVERYBODY WINS

Swedish society does pride itself on everyone being equal, with the exception of the Royal Family, and this does seem to stem from people being taught as kids that nobody loses. Sitting in shock, I was amazed to watch a televised children's quiz show where nobody lost despite someone obviously coming last. It seemed to defeat the point of having a competition in the first place and televising it to the whole country. Ok, so there was first place, the winner; second place, the runner up; third place, we'll call that bronze; fourth place, you actually sucked and came in last, but we can't possibly say that so… I tell you what, you win too, ok? All of the kids got the same trophy at the end of the show, and all of them were congratulated and praised for how well they had done. They were all smiling. Even the kid that failed miserably and came in last was smiling. There seemed to be no consequences at all for not doing well at this particular quiz. Now, compare this to England where if you suck at something and finish in last place, you are ridiculed by fellow classmates, told by teachers that you should try a bit harder, even though you suck and couldn't possibly do any better even if you were pumped with performance enhancing drugs. This invariably leads to ending up collecting the wooden spoon, and receiving a wedgy in the changing rooms.

Keeping on the theme of hardly any consequences, we can move onto the subject of detentions and expelling students. These things hardly ever happen in Sweden and troublesome students are usually sorted out with a call to the parents in the hope that they will sort their troublesome bundle(s) of joy out by giving them a stern talking to. It's against the law for anyone to dish out punishment in the form of a good hiding, preferring reasoning and common sense to rule the day, unless the parents are as crazy as their child is. In the UK, a clip round the ear and being sent to your room without any dinner is more commonplace although this is changing.

MEET THE TEACHERS

I remember all too well my parents going into school

on parents' night, meeting all my subject teachers to get a run down on what I was doing right, what I was doing wrong, and what I wasn't doing at all. It was a chance for them to meet some of the teachers that I hadn't kindly described. My parents always eyed me with caution and commented:

"Surely there can't be a teacher like that!"

After going to a parents' evening, they always came back with the confirmation of:

"Oh yes there can!" or "you were right."

Things might have changed back in good ol' Blighty since I was a youngster, but this was the experience I had when it came to parents' evening. Parents' evening in Sweden means just that. It's when all the parents of the students have a meeting together to keep them updated on school information. The parents' evening that is more similar to the English version is called a development meeting where the parents and the student meet the form teacher. When compared to the UK, a student gets an evening home alone, unless babysat, anxiously waiting for their parents to get back with either smiles or grimaces on their faces. To further fire home and reiterate what the teachers have said, in the UK, report cards are given to the parents to bring home with them so that there is no getting out of what's been said. This was my experience of the UK school system.

So, does the lack of losing, consequences, and report cards add up to a well-rounded, sensible individual that is ready for a working life after education is all said and done? To best answer this question, I'll invite you now to formulate your answer after reading the next paragraph.

A completely alien concept to most immigrants to Sweden is the graduation party that students throw after their time of studying at gymnasium has finally ended. Nothing wrong with a graduation party I hear you say, but there is a slight twist to what Swedish students actually do to blow off that pent up steam.

THE GUIDE TO SWEDISH STUDENT GRADUATION FOR IMMIGRANTS

STEP ONE

The first thing students do is buy a copious amount of alcohol.

Your projected reaction: Nothing strange there.

STEP TWO

The second thing they do is don their white, almost sailor like, graduation cap.

Your projected reaction: Not much wrong with that either.

STEP THREE

The third thing they do is to make banners and write on them the name of their class, school, and a slogan that reads something like,

- We're having a fest because we are best!

Your projected reaction: Again, this is perfectly reasonable to have a banner outside the hall where the party is. It's all above board so far.

STEP FOUR

The fourth thing they do is to look for a lorry to hire.

Your projected reaction: Ok. Now this is getting slightly strange. What's the lorry for? Surely students would rent a bus or coach to take them to the hall with the banners outside it?

STEP FIVE

The fifth thing they do, after they have rented the truck is to pin the banners to it, carry the alcohol on board and cram the class onto the back of the lorry with birch tree branches as decorations. It's also around this time where the drinking starts and the cheap foamy beers start spraying.

Your projected reaction: Now this is starting to get weird. What are they doing on a lorry? Somebody answer that question.

STEP SIX

The sixth thing they do is to start up some hideous poppy, dancy, techo music and turn up the volume as loud as they can and start their journey around the village, town, or city where they have studied. If they can shout and scream over the top of the loud music, then this is what they do too.

Your projected reaction: Erm. Ok. And the reason for this again is what exactly?

This is what students do after graduating, and as much as I have tried to understand the concept of letting the whole world know they have finished studying, and that they have graduated, I still don't understand why they do it. And it's not just me either. Many ex-pats from Britain and, in fact other countries, look on as these truckloads of inebriated hopes for the future drive past, shouting at anybody who looks, or doesn't look, in their direction. The first thing that immigrants will usually think and probably say out loud is:

- Yes. We know you've graduated. Get over it.

It's a totally bizarre concept to probably everybody who isn't Swedish, but when compared to Britain, you can understand why. A shake of the hand, the presentation of your diploma, goodbye party for the students, and the intention of staying in touch is all that happens in the UK.

Is there alcohol? Of course.

Are there caps? Only after graduating from university, only for a limited time, and not at the party.

Banners? Again, maybe. Depends if someone has been delegated to do it.

The rental of a lorry? No chance.

Shouting about the fact that you have graduated? No. Britain is still pretty conservative remember.

Poppy, dancy techno? There is a strong possibility some bad music will be heard and played at the party, but the alcohol would have numbed the ex-students' senses to it, leaving them immune to its effect.

As much as non-Swedes will tut and mumble their disapproval about noisy students, packed in like sardines on backs of lorries, new Swedish graduates will, no doubt, continue this tradition of getting wasted whilst shouting their celebratory message across the hemisphere.

WHAT YOU HAVE LEARNT FROM THIS CHAPTER

- Bears do not have to attend school, university, or climb onto the back of a lorry.

- Homework marked with a tick means failure.

- Swedish pupils are equal and always win even if they lose.

- Swedish teachers are softies.

- Finger biscuits are oddly shaped.

- Margaret Thatcher hated milk.

- If you spot or hear a lorry driving towards you, playing dodgy techno, filled with screaming graduates in white hats, avoid it.

5. WORK

To quote a famous song, work is just a four-letter word, and is something that virtually everybody can't avoid. I had moved with the equivalent of 500 pounds back in 2003, and was under the illusion that getting a job in Sweden wouldn't be that hard. A conversation with a couple on the plane over to Sweden didn't convince me it was difficult either. It wasn't until they both looked at me, shocked at my optimism, that it dawned on me that, perhaps, it would be more of challenge than I gave it credit for.

JOB AGENCIES

After I had moved, my faith was restored after I noticed that the same job agencies existed in Sweden. They would surely help a fresh immigrant to the country, I thought, as I made my way into one particular agency. After I had walked into the building, two staff members behind the reception frowned at me. There were no signs of life apart from them and the lights had been dimmed probably to save on electricity.

"Kan vi hjälpa dig?" asked one of the assistants.

"Oh, sorry. I can't speak Swedish. I'm just interested in finding work."

"Oh. I see. Well. You need to sign up online. Everything is there."

"Online? Can't I sign up here?"

"No, we don't do anything here."

"Oh."

I felt slightly flummoxed and perturbed and left in some state of confusion. In my home town, it was normal practice that a job agency would sign you up, tell you what jobs they had going and checked if you wanted to do any of them or not. I had never been to a job agency's office where the people that worked there didn't actually do anything. However, a job agency did call me after I had filled in their online form. I was going to an interview. At last, I was being considered for a job or so I thought. It was an exciting time as I needed to find work and an interview had to be good news, or so I thought. After I had answered all of their questions and showed them my portfolio, I then asked them what kind of job they had lined up for me to which they replied that they just wanted to put a face to a name. Put a face to a name? Were they kidding? I had wasted an hour of my life that I would never get back because they wanted to put a face to a name. I never did hear back from them.

ARBETSFÖRMEDLINGEN

I put the failings of job agencies behind me and de-cided to tackle the job centre instead as they would surely put me on the right track. Unbeknown to me, I made the mistake of turning up at 9.10 a.m. instead of 9 a.m. sharp. I took my number ticket and waited.. and waited.. and waited. An hour passed. To keep my blood circulating, I decided to look on the job data-base to see if I could find any job that might suit me.

Web developer.

Database master.

Acrobat.

Graphic designer.

Photogr…

Hold on a minute.. .. Acrobat? I kept scrolling,

Layout artist.

Clown.

Copywriter.

3D graphic…

Hold on a minute.. Clown?

Out of curiosity, I clicked on the clown job and read the description. It turned out that a clown was needed to entertain at children's parties. What kind of qualifications would you need to get a clown's job? Would you need a CV written in invisible ink? Turn up to an interview and squirt the boss in the face with a plastic flower? Throw custard pies at every employee on your way out?

After applying for several jobs off the job centre's website, I put my feet up and waited. After a short while, I was invited to some interviews fairly quickly, which was beyond my expectations.

As it turned out, my odd experience with agency interviews continued as I soldiered on with my quest of finding work in Sweden. The first interview I had took place on the top floor of the Lipstick building (named after its lipstick shape by Gothenburgers) in Gothenburg with a company that I had been in touch with to, maybe, organise some work experience. It wasn't a job but at least it was something, I thought, as I met the boss I had been exchanging emails with.

The boss asked me what I knew about the company, to which I had no answer. The boss started to become irritated and urged me to come back when I knew more about them. This was a hard task as the company was brand new and their website had no information on it whatsoever. I had actually checked what information existed on this particular company beforehand and this drew a blank. It was therefore lucky that they had sent a PDF with information on it for me to read. However, when I tried to open the file, my protective virus checker kicked in and detected that the PDF actually contained a virus. When I mentioned that fact to the boss, he treated me with more disrespect claiming that it sounded ridiculous that his precious PDF contained a virus. I lasted less than five minutes in the company of a boss who clearly expected miracles, and exited the Lipstick building, using more time than my interview had lasted.

My next interview was the complete reverse of this scenario. The company was situated just outside of Gothenburg, and I had arrived to the interview only to find the person who was to interview me had called in sick. It wasn't a problem as somebody else would do it instead. As the interview ticked into an hour, I knew what the job was about, what it would require, what flavours of tea were available to me, and where the fire exits were. As the interview ticked into two hours, I knew what the interviewer's hobby of martial arts was all about, how to make a keyboard sound like a guitar, and the ins and outs of mass communication theory attached to websites. As the interview ticked close into its third hour, I knew what the interviewer's pet dog was called, what his wife did in her spare time, and the pin-code to his bank card. It was at this point I calmly asked: "when do I start?" He had obviously kept me there for half a morning for a reason. When he started to stutter back to me, I soon realised that this probably wasn't one of my best moves, and he said he couldn't make any decision. I left the premises after almost three hours and was certain that I had that job in the bag, but was surprised when I heard that the company had gone bust two weeks later. It was yet another huge chunk out of my life that I'll never get back again, and another job interview that I've never been able to understand.

Swedish job interviews are, of course, to be taken seriously in the same way that English job interviews are, but there is something more casual about them. Sometimes wearing posh clothes to one would be considered over the top by Swedish standards depending on the position, opting more for the smart but casual approach. This can be unsettling for the standard Brit who expects to turn up in their Sunday best to stand a good chance of getting the job.

Sweden's calm, casual but smart approach can lure a Brit into a false sense of security, thinking that the interviewers have suddenly become your friends and that you can calmly chat to them about anything. It's funny how a small change can do so much damage.

Cold calling is perfectly acceptable and is said to be one of the best ways to find a job in Sweden. Most job adverts found on the job centre's website come with a contact number and urge you to call if you have any questions. Compared to England, you send off a letter and CV and hope for the best. That's all there is to it.

If strange job descriptions and bizarre job interviews are sucking you into the vortex of the Swedish job market, a black hole could await you if you unlucky to take just any job offer that comes your way. There are a large number of lone agents and extremely small companies, as with any country, with less than approximately five people, that might offer you some work. For the sake of argument, we'll call this group of people cowboys. I have been sucked into this black hole myself, and can say from first hand experience that if you take this kind of job, you might well be scratching your head after three months, trying to figure out when you will get paid. It's unfortunate that this happens but it nevertheless does, and isn't contained to just Sweden either.

Trade unions have more of a presence than they do in England. They were stomped out in the '80s leaving them virtually powerless to do anything about bad working conditions and start to wave white flags when trouble rears its head. Unions in Sweden, however, are set up to help everybody from workers to managers to whole companies. Not every company will welcome them with open arms, but if Swedish law has been followed along with company policy, then there shouldn't be any problems for a union to sort out.

In terms of a normal working person, unions can offer all kinds of services including grants for studying, job coaches, and most importantly, something called A-kassa. Briefly explained, A-kassa is an insurance scheme where you pay a monthly fee and if you are laid off or out of work, you can claim benefits up to 80% of your wage. Different A-kassas will have their own rules and regulations. 80% of your wage is unheard of in England, and if you are laid off, the benefits you receive are at a minimum. There is also an A-kassa that is separate from the unions so if, for some crazy reason, you don't want to be a member of a union, you can still sign up to A-kassa.

THE JOB

Once you have your feet over the door, down the hallway, past the snacks machine, and under the desk, what can you expect from the Swedish way of working? Efficient Swedish time keeping is one thing you can expect but in connection with meetings. Lots of them. If you work within a small organisation, you can expect fewer of them compared to a large company, but nevertheless, Swedes like meetings. They'll have meetings on time schedules, meetings on how things are going, meetings on how you are doing, meetings on company matters and meetings about meetings. You'll end up going to so many meetings that the work you got employed to do won't ever have a chance of getting done. To combat this, a meeting about meetings will go over the fact that the amount of meetings is just ludicrous and that they'll be scaled down so there will be less of them. The only problem with having a meeting about meetings is that further meetings will be scheduled to check how the fewer amount of proposed meetings has worked out for you, adding further meetings into your calendar. In the UK, back in my old job, I worked for a large company for almost seven years, and can you guess how many meetings took place? The answer? Zero. I went through one development dialogue during my time at my previous employer and that was it. Obviously, it all depends on if you include all the meetings we had at the pub over the road at lunchtimes. Hiccup!

If you have escaped all of those meetings, and you are sitting at your desk, why not stand instead? Most companies, these days, have invested in ergonomic chairs and desks that you can raise or lower to improve posture and avoid thrombocythemia. It's the norm within Swedish organisations but does come with one problem. If you want to raise your desk because you are fed up with sitting down like a chump, you might want to check the desk of the person next to you before you raise yours as accidents can happen. The cup of coffee you have placed on your desk that just goes over the boundary between your neighbour's desk could end up splashing itself over a computer keyboard near you and it will probably be yours. It's hard to avoid getting the odd coffee cup stamp of approval on some paperwork, but the whole content of a cup is something you certainly don't want. I remember raising my desk for the first time, looking in horror as my cup of coffee decided to lose its balance and deposit its content on my MacBook Pro. Small bubbles of air popped from my keyboard as I watched the liquid slowly start to soak into the fairly expensive piece of technology. Frantically trying to rescue the situation and save my computer, a trickle of coffee dripped out of the Mac when I held it upside down in a vain attempt to keep it alive. You know what? It worked. My MacBook Pro not only survived the tidal wave of caffeine, it actually worked better afterwards. There's an advert for coffee if there ever is one.

Meetings and coffee stains are commonplace in most businesses whether you live in the UK or Sweden but fruit is not. UK businesses may well have an old, slightly broken, vending machine that will throw you out something that resembles warm mud in a cup, but Swedish businesses will have fresh fruit every morning. Up and down the country, early in the mornings, fruit is being delivered to most businesses in Sweden, with the people who start early getting a jump on those who start later. This can happen to such a degree that anyone who starts their day at 10 a.m. will be out of luck in the fruit fetching stakes. It's just the way it is. Bananas are the root of all work related crimes against fruit hoarding, and it's the humble banana that will disappear the quickest. There have been many theories to why bananas are taken more than the other fruits including; they are easy to carry in your pocket; they don't cause stitches if you exercise after eating one; you won't get a banana lodged in your upper dentures like you will with an apple.

I can't explain the reason why fruit is delivered in straw baskets to Swedish businesses. There's certainly nothing wrong with the fruit itself. It's not old, mouldy, or looks as if someone has played fruit football in a warehouse with it. It's just something Swedes do. This also applies to something called Friday *fika* where businesses will order in cakes and pastry items in an effort to make employees socialise a little bit on a Friday afternoon. At one company where I worked, there were no standards or quality control on the cakes as there had been on the fruit. The cakes could either be fancy or ropey. There's no middle ground here and again, the quicker you are to the cake, the more chance you have at stealing a slice. People who say they will make it later in the afternoon as they have too much to do will probably be the people who also missed out on the fruit earlier. If you are making it to the company canteen at 4 p.m., then you will probably find a silver cardboard sheet, a small blob of whipped cream accompanied by crumbs as your prize. The early Swede catches the fruit and cakes.

In the UK, the Friday afternoon *fika* is replaced by the Friday liquid lunch for many, where bosses will give permission for a longer lunch break, and then join later themselves. This is really the English equivalent to *fika* Friday, and instead of cakes, we like to say it with beer instead, going back to work half sloshed, and trying to use a computer that seemed a lot easier to use beforehand.

Coffee is discharged out of machines within most companies, and fruit might be the difference between Swedish and UK businesses, but is there anything else the Swedes do? Yes. Parents of new bundles of joy into the world can get 480 days parental leave. My inquisitive relatives usually respond with a "bloody hell" when I relay this information. The 480 days can be shared and split between the parents - "bloody hell". The days can also be taken at any time up until a child has turned eight years old - "bloody hell". It's no wonder Sweden is in the top ten of countries with the best quality of life.

Employees can also leave for a year and keep their job open at the same time. Although unpaid, this is also something that is unheard of in the UK. Usually, a person has to leave their job to do something else, and if their job is still available by the time they come back, then great, otherwise it's back to the job centre again.

If you are moving house, or flat, no problem! Swedes have this covered too with a day off work to help you do it. They obviously won't help you with the move, and lay on removal men to shift heavy beds and sofas, but maybe that is next on the cards. Bearing in mind the amount of times you might have to move if you are renting a property in Stockholm, these days really do come in handy, and is something that doesn't happen in the UK. If you are moving house in the UK, you really have to do that in your own time or book a day off to do it.

So, besides 480 days parental leave, a year's leave, a day off for moving, coffee, free fruit, and cakes on a Friday, what have the Swedes ever done for their workers? Discounts for healthy exercise, that's what! If you weren't already content with all of the above, then most companies will also chuck in a set amount of money for you to use against costs for doing something healthy in your leisure time. For most, this will mean joining a gym. Some will have varying amounts of cash to lob at you if you decide to use it but most will do it. The Swedes really have taken a leaf out the Romans' book here with this, realising that a happy worker will produce the best results. In the UK, the boss buying you a beer is seen as one of the perks of the job when compared, and there really isn't anything like this in the UK that I have seen.

If the discount can't sway you, the time off is not enough, the cakes have not weighed you down or the fruit has all been eaten, or hoarded by early birds, then you are either ungrateful or wanting to change jobs. In the UK, the bog standard resignation is in written form and requires a month's notice. After a month, your fellow colleagues will have had a whip-round, gone out and bought an embarrassing present, followed up by a night down the pub to really say goodbye. In Sweden, the same resignation letter is required, but usually with three months notice, depending on how long you have worked at one particular place. Three months notice is a long time, and it will seem like an eternity before you can actually leave the workplace. By the time you get to the last month, and, depending on what sort of person you are, you will be probably be zapped of all energy knowing a new start is not so very far away. If you put this into the context of all those meetings that I described earlier, a company may well choose to carry on treating you as if that three months notice and resignation didn't exist. Take, for example, a story of a friend of mine who handed in his resignation. He was invited to the same meetings right up until the bitter end where deadlines didn't apply to him anymore. They still asked him for his input anyway as if his resignation was just a bit of a joke, and checked if the goodbye fika was still happening too. He didn't mean it. He'll be here next week right?

THINGS YOU HAVE LEARNT FROM THIS CHAPTER

• Bears could be stealing the free fruit.

• Job agencies just want to be friends.

• A clown is a job for life, not just for kids' parties.

• A three-hour job interview is no indication of sure employment.

• Clothes do not maketh the man.

• Problems with cowboys and Indians can be solved with unions, otherwise known as sheriffs.

• After you have read this chapter, let's have a meeting to find out what you have learnt and then sum that up in a meeting afterwards.

• Do a cup check before raising an electric desk.

• Free fruit. Free cakes. Time off. Training discount. What else do you want?

• Resignations are to be ignored until you have actually left.

6. MUSIC

Sweden has been responsible for many bands that have hit the big time. The obvious ones would be ABBA, Roxette, The Cardigans, Björn Ranelid. Sweden has also been responsible for lesser-known bands that helped shaped music. In the prog rock world, Sweden had Hansson and Karlsson that were deemed to be so good that Jimi Hendrix recorded a cover of their song *Tax Free*, as well as playing it live on a number of occasions. The Soundtrack Of Our Lives that hail from Gothenburg have supported Brit bands like Oasis, for example, on tours and one of their songs appeared in an episode of CSI:NY. Have you heard the song that starts with: "Ooga chucka Ooga Ooga chucka… I can't stop this feeling…"? Although a cover version, the well-known version is Swedish and features Björn Skifs on vocals.

REHEARSAL ROOMS

It's estimated that in Gothenburg alone, there are between 1,500-2,000 unsigned bands floating around, all jostling for gigs and to be heard. I'm not sure what the number is for Stockholm but I would imagine that it would probably be above those figures. So with all these bands, how on earth do they all get to practice and play live?

I have played bass since 1994, and I know that musicians are made to suffer for their art in the UK. If my hometown is anything to judge standards by, every practice room that I have ever played in has been a disused, cold, dark building with just enough plug sockets to go around. Some people dispensed with these places and just tried to jam at home or find somewhere at work that might suffice. Of course, nothing suffices when you have angry neighbours knocking on your door and are threatening you. It's also not so good to jam in a place where the ceiling flakes on you because of the noise. So when compared, Sweden is actually a breeze when organising a practice session or gig.

There are many associations that help music artists and bands get those practice sessions up and running and many will have practice rooms set up with timetables where you can book yourself in. When I walked into my first practice room, I was surprised and found differences straight away:

They used light bulbs in the ceiling to illuminate the room.

They had central heating.

They had fairly good equipment that seemed to be in working order.

The room had equipment full stop.

The room didn't smell of the sweat of the previous occupants.

You had trouble hearing the other bands playing.

The premises had a rest area with a coffee and snack machine.

It didn't cost a fortune.

I certainly wasn't used to this kind of luxury and I quickly realised that maybe Swedes felt that music was really important to them. If the above points weren't doing it for you then how would a discount in the music shops feel? How would playing at a few venues in town feel? When I first got a few work-mates to jam, we just wanted to use the room to play some covers and muck around to relieve some stress from a working day. After a month of doing this, the leader of this particular association and practice room wanted to hear us and said:

"You must be ready to gig now – let's hear what you have got".

I didn't know what to say so I just said that we were just practicing and didn't have anything at all really. This sheer level of enthusiasm would take most bands in England aback, but as we weren't doing anything of a serious nature, I had to beat him back with an imaginary stick. Later on, after I had joined another band, and helped another, I soon realised how helpful these associations were to the music community in Sweden and wished they existed in England.

IN THE KEY OF H

However, once I had joined a Swedish band, my first practice session wasn't without hiccups. If you have read the language chapter in this book, then you'll remember how I said that you'd have to learn how to tell the time again. The same almost happened with music. The Swedes have also managed to make this slightly confusing. If you play guitar, the strings are as follows E, A, D, G, B, E and that, I thought, was standard everywhere. Not so. Sweden, as well as other countries, has the note H. I'm not making this up. Every musician in the UK everywhere will probably be jumping up and down as they read this thinking that they have been missing out on a secret note that has revolutionised music. I'll save all of you from wetting your pants in excitement by simply saying that they have taken B and called it H instead. Not only do Swedes make you learn how to tell the time again, take your shoes off at the front door, and turn your barcodes away from cashiers, they have also made a UK immigrant musician's life harder with the note H.

GIGS

Once you have mastered H, you might well be at the level to go gigging. I have played a few gigs around Sweden and there hasn't been an establishment that won't serve you food if you are playing that evening. Some establishments serve up some good food. It's sometimes not a case of them giving you a burger and saying - get on with it, but more a case of - you are our guests. Here's some salmon, potatoes and veg for you. Again, pure luxury, and, of course, you get discounts on drinks too, just to ram home that VIP feeling.

What about the gigs themselves? Some venues are better than others and some gigs go better than others, nothing out of the ordinary there. The Swedish music loving public is something different altogether. Music fans in Sweden seem to actually absorb tunes at a gig rather than dance, jump up and down and go crazy. At one particular gig, where the popular Swedish band Kent was playing, the crowd figure was said to have been 1,000+ people. I stood quite close to the front, and the band played their usual brand of indie pop rock to their fans with just a small section of fans jumping up and down, shouting their lyrics back at them.

A phenomenon that happens with some Swedish audiences is for them not to move much at all, stand fairly still, rub their chin and evaluate what that particular song has just done for them. It takes a while for a large crowd to warm up to bands and, therefore, bands have to work just that little bit harder to melt the ice. This changes when alcohol enters the picture and there are festivals to go to.

THE OLDER AND TRADITIONAL SWEDISH MUSIC

One type of music that does break the ice is traditional Swedish music and it doesn't matter if you are into rap, rock or pop, it seems the Swedes will join hands, wave their lighters and sing old folk songs. It all has to do with childhood memories and traditions. The songs have got such a pull that most will be sung at either Skansen, the outdoor museum in Stockholm, or Liseberg, the fairground in Gothenburg, and will be televised, with lyric subtitles if you want to sing-a-long at home if you couldn't make it to either of those places. I've even seen someone wearing a Metallica t-shirt singing along. It's a bizarre thing to have to witness if you are not Swedish and it takes some getting used to as well some understanding. The closest the UK came to this was the TV show *Songs Of Praise* where hymns were sung in a church, mostly by pensioners, with subtitled hymn texts all about religion. Well, it was shown on Sundays, and it was called *Songs Of Praise* after all. Usually, in my family, if we caught the last 5 minutes of this show, we would have a competition to count how many people were wearing glasses to make the five minutes pass quicker. Call me a heathen if you want to. I'll let you.

Traditional music is one thing, but there is something else that happens in Sweden that just can't be explained: stars and celebs from the past who keep on touring despite not being able to sing as well as they could in the '50s and '60s. It's going back to that concept of nobody loses in Sweden. Yes, of course you can still get up on stage and sing all those old songs that people still like, even though you don't sound as good as you did and a tad shaky. The UK, however, is not devoid of old stars like Cliff Richard who still tours frequently, but at least he can still hold notes down and the same can be said for Paul McCartney who still has that Beatle magic. It's hard to say why old music artists still perform when they probably shouldn't, but maybe it's because they have been around a long time and still have the big personas they had back in the day when they were really popular.

DANSBAND

If singing traditional songs is one thing and old stars singing is another, there is one form of music that is sinister to say the least. There is no explanation to what contribution dansband music makes to Sweden. For those of you who don't know what dansband is, get comfortable, pour yourself something strong and get ready to be shocked and paralysed.

Cast your mind back to the UK in the '70s and, perhaps '80s, and dredge up a memory of a band called Showaddywaddy. Remember them? If you don't, just look them up and study a group photo of them. Done that? Good. Now imagine that picture with them wearing outfits worse than those and imagine how they might sound and you have a fair idea of what dansband is all about.

What I believed to be a unique concept to Sweden soon turned out to be popular in other countries like Germany as well. Old songs sung in a country, pop-way by artists that looked as if they had their costumes supplied by the clothes left behind by old American country bands of the '60s and '70s. There was probably a vintage country music clothing store that was in danger of being closed down until dansband started up in Sweden.

These bands are called dansband because that is essentially what they are there to do, play old songs at a folkpark, a venue that exists in almost every Swedish town. The aim of a dansband is for people to, well, dance to their music. No problem there really as it's just supposed to be fun at the end of the day, right? Instead of this form of music being contained like a virus, it leaked out into the general public and, somehow, started to become popular.

Horrified as I was, I couldn't, and still can't, understand why this form of music is still popular in Sweden, especially when it starts crossing into the mainstream. Even if I try to ignore the horrific costumes that some of them wear, the cheesy way they act sometimes, and the way they sing the songs, still doesn't make me understand the pull towards them. It's all a matter of taste I guess. For some people, dansband provide light entertainment that you don't have to think about, but for many they provide entertainment through them just looking and sounding cheesy. Not all dansband will look as if they have been sucked out of a time warp from the country music scene in the '70s. Some modern dansband have chosen to ditch the uniformed, clown-like costumes and opted for some more sensible dress instead. Unfortunately, their music still sounds similar to that of their contemporaries but at least it is a step in the right direction.

If dansband music had been confined to the folk-park, where I assume it came from, it would have been fine and dandy, but instead, we have to endure dansband music through album adverts, appearances on morning shows and, even worse, Melodifestivalen. So just when you think it's safe to take the ear-plugs out, you'll be scrambling to cement them back in again.

THINGS YOU HAVE LEARNT FROM THIS CHAPTER

- Bears don't listen to music, as they can't find head sets large enough for their heads.

- Practice rooms are lit, tidy, and don't smell.

- You'll be gigging before learning any songs.

- You might be asked to play a song in the key of H.

- Swedish music fans are sonic sponges.

- Traditional songs turn the hardest metal head into putty.

- Singing out of tune is not necessarily a disadvantage.

- Dansband may look cuddly but will attack you with classic old songs that have been butchered.

7. FOOD AND DRINK

Before I go any further with this chapter, divulging information on Swedish food and drink habits, I just want to mention the Swedish chef. The Muppet Show may have been responsible for putting Swedish cuisine, and its rhythmic language, on some kind of map but it's way too old now and way too easy to start doing "hooby doo" impressions. Now that's out of the way, we can start delving into the nitty gritty of food and drink in Sweden and what better way to start than to talk about tea & coffee.

TEA & COFFEE

The English are famed for their love of tea and have been since their tongues first came into contact with it. Tea is the drink that really brings people together in England, and it solves every problem that could pop up during a day, no matter how serious it may be. If someone is arguing with somebody else, an innocent bystander may well say:

- Let's all have a cup of tea.

If somebody has just been burgled and had all the valuables taken from their house, a friend or near relative might say:

- Let's have a cup of tea.

Even if someone has had a relative pass on, you might hear:

- Let's have a cup of tea.

You see, in England, tea makes everything better. Forget plasters. Forget therapy sessions. Forget your own sadness or bad situation you have got yourself into to. Tea is the answer and if you're not drinking at least fifteen cups a day, staining your teeth brown and rotting them quicker than pears in a fruit bowl, then there is something wrong with you.

Although the UK is famed for their tea drinking, we have become accustomed to using the bag, and loose tealeaves are something of a rare sight these days. It's therefore odd to see Sweden offering all varieties of loose tea in the shops plus a multitude of teabags that would put England to shame. In fact, the choice of flavours in bag and loose forms far outweighs anything I have seen in the UK. You could say us Brits are spoilt for choice in a nation that really prefers coffee over tea any day of the week.

Swedes love their coffee and drink it by the barrel over breakfast, a keg load over lunch, and brewery load during the day. They can't get enough of it. Although instant coffee, which is so popular in the UK, is available in Sweden, it's the freshly ground or bean variety that sells the most with the instant kind being largely frowned upon. It's come to the point where electrical goods shops sell a whole range of coffee makers: bog standard filter machines; small espresso makers that you warm up on hot plates; coffee presses; huge industrial espresso machines for the ardent coffee drinker and new-fangled capsule machines that take, what look to be, small packets of hotel milk. I'm sure they'll invent a coffee intravenous soon.

My very first experience of coffee dates way back to my arrival in Gothenburg when I was killing time, wandering about in Central Station. After walking through the same flower shop for the fourth time, I was ambushed by a guy wearing a green uniform, carrying a flamethrower. I thought it might have been a unique way to bake the cinnamon buns I could smell, but instead the guy spoke to me whilst keeping a thumb on the trigger:

"Lite kaffe?"

"Sorry? I don't speak Swedish."

"Ah. Sorry. Would you like some coffee?" said the guy, thrusting a small plastic cup in my face.

The canister on his back was similar to the ones

that insect busters use when fumigating a house. Unless I was mistaken, he was going to insect bust my cup with a free sample of coffee. A quick splash and dash later, my cup was filled with the latest coffee and the guy went on his merry way, making sure that he splashed out a few more cups for nearby unsuspecting people. As I watched the ghostbuster disappear, I took a sip of the coffee and decided that his canister probably had been filled with insect-killer, as it tasted repulsive. Thankfully, now after tasting other coffee, this was just a one-off free sample that had lost a potential sale.

BREAKFAST

Coffee is served up alongside breakfast, which usually consists of a variety of different things being spread out over several plates. Porridge. Cheese. Ham. Maybe more than one type of bread. Orange juice. Two types of spread. Eggs. It was a different way of having breakfast from what I was used to. Being a cereal killer, I always opted for a simple bowl of something that resembled rabbit hutch scrapings drenched in milk. It required no effort and could be eaten in less than ten minutes but this type of breakfast was something I had only encountered in hotels.

During my first breakfast, I liked the fact that I had choices as I chomped down some great tasting bread, washed down with real coffee, but just as I was getting comfortable, I was rudely awoken to one food that almost every Swede was addicted to. Raw fish. Now, being a fan of sushi, this didn't immediately put me off, but I was curious about a jar of pickled herring that I carefully examined. After I had opened the jar, it didn't smell too bad, and it had been pickled in onion and pepper. Flapping down a small piece of herring onto my bread, I thought the best way to tackle it would be to eat the whole thing without chewing, which I did to some degree of success. It was like Fear Factor but with raw fish dressed up as food.

KALLES KAVIAR

Herring passed my test and it was added to my diet, but the next item, however, would turn into an experience that was almost indescribable. It was a blue tube of caviar that featured a smiley blonde boy on it that looked as if it had been drawn in the '50s. I had only seen caviar in small jars, priced up beyond the reach of any normal working class citizen, but here was the Swedish version, in a tube, with a smiley kid looking at me, almost winking. It certainly looked harmless enough and if the smiley kid was winking and telling me that it was tasty, I couldn't really argue. It was suggested that I try a small blob on a boiled egg as this was the nectar of all Swedes and how everyone usually ate it.

I opened the tube and inhaled through my nose. It smelt vile. Not really paying attention to one of my five senses I, very foolishly, blobbed a small bit of caviar onto my egg. It looked vile. I likened it to strawberry toothpaste that had lost its way and really let itself go. I would have much preferred the strawberry toothpaste on my egg as I eyed up the now soiled boiled egg looking at me from my plate. I ignored two of my five senses and decided that the Fear Factor non-chew method was the way to go. I picked up the egg and put the whole thing in my mouth. As the cold, fishy paste hit my tongue, I started to shiver and all the hairs on the back of my neck down to my buttocks stood up on end. This food was violating me and there was nothing I could do about it. Squinting and grimacing at the breakfast table, I looked at the tube again and quickly scanned it for a government health warning. Nope. I couldn't find one. Even packets of cigarettes came with health risk warnings but this putrid combination of raw fish eggs and potato was, and still is, one of the worst tastes I have allowed onto my tongue.

A TV commercial for Kalles Kaviar featured the slogan "It's a very Swedish taste" after giving folks in Japan a sample taste of the fishy foe. The Japanese appeared not to like the taste either as they winced their way through the thirty seconds of madness.

This goes to show that even ABBA Seafood, the makers of Kalles Kaviar, know that this product is really just for the Swedes.

OTHER TUBED FOOD & THE RETURN OF KALLES KAVIAR

Unfortunately, my psyche has been tainted by the Kalles Kaviar experience to the point where I am now afraid of tubed food and there is a lot of it to be afraid of in Sweden. There are all kinds of variety of tubed cheese. For example, tubed cheese with shrimps, with bacon, with ham, with mushrooms, peppers, crab, moving onto more bizarre tubes of shrimp cheese with chili and oranges.

There isn't a combination of bizarre ingredients that can top what I am about to tell you now. Once upon a time, in a caviar factory some distance away, but not far, far away, a board meeting decided on a new flavour combination that would revolutionise the tubed caviar world. A combination that was so delicious in their minds, that they assumed it was going to be a sure-fire hit right across Sweden. A combination that no Swede would ever be able to resist and would become a drug of choice. The combination?

Banana and caviar.

I wish I were joking about this, but for a short time, the same caviar company developed and released banana caviar with the slogan "Trust us. It's good!" Figuring that they were the masters of caviar, they assumed that this combination was a real winner and would secure their financial future way into the year 3000. It wasn't fooling me. The original caviar had left me with a bad taste in my mouth three years earlier, and there was no way anyone could add a special ingredient to jazz it up when the original already tasted worse than my own vomit. Just when I thought it was safe to go into my own fridge, something even more putrid had crept in. Trust them? I'd rather take my chances with raw chicken thanks.

LUNCH

Lunch in Sweden is all about a hot meal and not the sandwiches that are much revered in England and, in fact, Denmark and Norway. The rules also change with your drink of choice too, as I found out when I ordered a tea with my pizza, much to the shocked and amazed faces of my newfound Swedish friends. I had to ask them if this was at all strange to which they replied, in a diplomatic fashion, that most people would order a cold drink with their pizza rather than a tea. In my defence, I blamed the fact that I ate sandwiches for lunch in the UK and, therefore, any drink came into play and being English, my drink of choice was tea. I had no idea that I was going to be judged on my order of hot drinks at lunchtime but there you go.

Throwing the hot versus cold drink argument to the side, Sweden is a nation of lunch deals, and it sometimes pays to wander around and find the best one. If you are living in a city, it's often warfare when you walk past restaurants and cafés with price deals as weaponry. Whether you are Swedish or an immigrant, there is nothing more pleasing and satisfying than bragging to friends that you have found the lunch deal to beat all lunch deals. Usually the conversation will end up with you saying that the deal costs 65 kronor and they throw in an apple! Just that mention of a piece of cheap fruit will swing it for most of your friends as they barge you out of the way and head to the pearl you have just discovered.

SEAFOOD

There's nothing strange about Swedish dinners but when it comes to special occasions, there is nothing that quite prepares you for new techniques in eating some of it.

Sweden basically eats any sealife that happens to get caught up in a net or caught on the end of a rod somewhere, excluding endangered species. My childhood memories were always haunted by my grandma opening cans of salmon to spread on our sandwiches and then, presumably, we would eat them after checking the sell by date and declaring them safe. After I had tried salmon and realising how different it tastes in Sweden, when compared to my grandma's tinned preference, it became something I added to the shopping list. However, eating salmon is not a complex and hard thing to do but there is some seafood that exists that should come with a handbook.

My hometown of Northampton is the furthest away from any given coastline in the UK and when we consider the simple shrimp, it usually comes ready peeled and may have the chance of giving you food poisoning which, unfortunately, some of my friends have experienced. No monkey business like that happens in Sweden because fresh shrimps are available from almost anywhere, but there is a price to pay. You have to learn how to peel them.

The best way to approach a shrimp is to first twist off the head and detach it. Try to ignore the eyes that look like black pepper kernels, and place the head in a vacant bowl. We'll call it the carcass bowl for now although this name will change soon. Then twist off the tail and peel away the rest of the shell-like material that surrounds the meaty bit that you want to keep. Place all the freshly twisted off parts in the carcass bowl and the meaty goodness in another bowl. We'll call this the meaty goodness bowl. Keep repeating the above steps until your carcass bowl has turned into a pyramid of unwanted shrimp parts. Rename the carcass bowl to the pyramid bowl. Once you have got this stage, you'll notice that the unwanted parts largely outweigh the meaty goodness you were expecting to have more of. You'll get used to this. After all, there really isn't much meat on a shrimp. Once you have washed your hands, you can get to work in devouring the shrimps on bread combined with a squeeze of lemon and, maybe, mayonnaise if you want.

WARNING: This is only step one in obtaining your black belt in figuring out how to eat shelled seafood.

The next tricky crustacean is a real puzzle and not even Ernő Rubik could have invented or devised something so fiendishly hard. The crayfish. Around August/September is a bad time to be a crayfish because Swedes hold crayfish parties to generally crack open, consume, and suck dry these once water-loving beasties. I was introduced to crayfish within my first year of living in Sweden and it's a hard thing to comprehend. The cray fish is served up complete and without being shelled and it's up to you to find out where all the meat is on this oversized hard shrimp or mini lobster. To really drive home the point that

these things are tough nuts to crack, a special implement is laid out on the table alongside your normal
knife and fork. Thin, long and shaped like a bayonet,
this tool is needed to scoop out any potential meat
that may want to stay attached to the body.

How do you go about eating a crayfish? There
doesn't seem to be an easy way into one of these
things. No little compartment or weak spot that will
magically make it shrug off its hard shell. The easiest
way to get into a crayfish is to make sure you are sitting next to a Swede who will show you how but if
that doesn't happen, I'll give you a quick lesson.

The first step is a gruesome one so if any veg-
etarians or vegans are reading, I would skip to the
next chapter if you haven't already. Step one is to
twist off the head to reveal the brains, which I have
been told is the best part so, if you enjoy eating some
brownish-orange, slimy goo this should be right up
your street. The second step is to twist off the claws,
which usually results in even the most hardy of
Swedes saying - ow - because they can be sharp and
prickly. After you are past the point of being jabbed
and spiked by the claws, you then break them in half
where the joint is, resulting in some stringy meat
protruding from the break. This is where the special
long fork implement comes into play, or not as the
case may be. Sometimes, you can use the fork to get
at the stringy meat inside the claws and some people
will persist in wrestling with this until they turn blue

in the face. Most, like myself, will have given up with this tool and opted to try to just suck out the meat with their mouths instead. Just cut out the middleman. When this doesn't work, sling the claws into the carcass/pyramid bowl that was described earlier. Hopefully, once you have cracked open the crayfish and taken out the meaty goodness in the same way you did with the shrimp, you should be left with a slightly larger shrimp-like piece of meat, a much larger pyramid of crayfish parts to throw away that you might even need two pyramid bowls, and maybe with some sweat on your forehead after all that effort. After you have repeated all of the above five or six times, you might have enough meat to make one sandwich with so it's up to you whether you feel the time invested will deliver a big enough reward.

If you want to achieve ninja status in eating seafood, then attempt to eat a crayfish that has been cooked in a stew or broth. The best way in attempting to eat a crayfish that has been cooked in this way is to obtain a radiation suit and hope wherever you are allows you to wear it. All the liquids that the crayfish has been cooked in will have soaked into it, turning it into a ticking time bomb when you try and crack it open. Most of the sauce will avoid entering your mouth and end up on your best shirt or dress, probably the people next to you, the ceiling and the floor. If you thought it was difficult to eat before, this elevates it to near impossible status.

SURSTRÖMMING aka FERMENTED HERRING

The Swedes are not just content with fresh fish and shelled Rubik's cubes of the deep. They also sell fermented fish in small, almost oval shaped tins. Although more associated with ancient times in the north of Sweden, the next type of seafood has a more acquired taste and is for the more adventurous diner. If you are not content with fighting shelling shrimps and disassembling crayfish, you may want to achieve your 1st dan in seafood with *surström-ming*, which translated means sour herring. Now, you might be forgiven for thinking that *surströmming* is a pushover to prepare because you don't have to twist heads, suck claws like straws or use fancy cutlery, but you'd be wrong and here's why. You have to remember that the herring has been nicely rotting for approximately two and a half months, placed inside a can and then shipped out to supermarkets. For those who live south of Östersund, *surströmming* is not particularly appetising, even for Swedes, so these cans can probably be on the supermarket shelves for a while. There's no real danger of the product going off because it's already that way when it's put on sale. By the time somebody gets around to plucking up the courage to actually consider buying a tin, the fermentation has caused the tin to bulge into the oval shape I described earlier. And herein lies the danger and the biggest problem of all, which is to consider what tactic to use to open the tin itself. Primed, loaded and ready to take out an eyeball, you really have to be careful when opening a tin of *surström-ming*. Opening a tin in your apartment or house is a big no-no and some apartment associations do not allow it at all. So what do you do if you want a taste of rotting sea life? Well, one way to do it is to open the can outside and in a bag so you'll be able to keep the use of your eyes but maybe not your sense of smell. The other way is to open the can underwater, which is probably the smartest way to do it although you'll still be able to smell it. The odour itself can be described as a strong sufuric hit, mixed with stagnant water with an underlying hint of something fishlike but not quite. Once you get past the sheer shock of smelling *surströmming*, you have to get past the fact that you are about to eat herring that's, well, off. Northern Swedes eat *surströmming* on tunnbröd (thin bread) with red onion, potato and, sometimes, crème fraiche. An all-important glass of milk should be kept nearby at all times and used in emergencies. You'll be glad to know that *surströmming* does not taste as bad as it smells and actually tastes like a really salty version of its healthier jarred version. It's not advisable to eat *surströmming* in the amount you would usually eat of the normal pickled herring but if you do and it all proves too much, you can turn to the glass of milk, which can also be called the hero of the day. The answer to the question - why? - can't

113

be clearly answered for anyone attempting to under-stand the consumption of two month old mouldy fish, but Swedes in the north will stand up and de-fend it as a tradition. Other Swedes, however, will say the northerners can keep it to themselves and are quite content with putrid tubed caviar instead even though, in my opinion, it tastes far worse, with or without the banana.

SPECIAL MEALS

Special occasions such as Midsummer and Christmas are always celebrated with special food. Swedes may like their food but they also like to watch others eat. The Nobel Prize Banquet is one of the highlights of the culinary world in Sweden, and the master chefs who prepare the meal are interviewed to reveal what the lucky guests will be served up. The whole ban-quet is televised live for several hours where speech-es will be given, performances will occur, and the Royals will digest. What will they be served up as a starter? What will the Royals be wearing? Where can I buy the cutlery? These are just some of the ques-tions some Swedes will ponder over as the chomping of the master chef meal commences. Again, a dinner like this probably wouldn't be televised in the UK, but it does have Last Night of the Proms and The Trooping of the Colour to compare it with, however different and unrelated to food they might be.

What about the special meals that conjure up memories, happy times and frivolity within families? In the UK, there's the Christmas meal and then there's the...well, the Christmas meal. That's all the UK has unless you prepare a special dinner for Easter and not everyone does that. Swedes have a special meal for most of the special times of year and one of these occasions is the Midsummer dinner.

The Midsummer (or midsommar in Swedish) platter usually includes the now infamous pickled herring, boiled fresh new potatoes with dill, cold sliced salmon, boiled eggs with fancier real caviar, a large amount of salad and strawberries and cream as a dessert. Add a shot of snapps to the mix and your Midsummer meal is complete. Swedes regard this meal as important as the Christmas meal and people generally desert their city or town abode to spend this time with family.

The main issue of contention over food comes at Christmas time, and if you are a foreigner, then this can become a major sticking point between couples.

If you come from the UK, then Christmas dinner is all about indulgence. You eat lots, you drink lots, you watch a lot of TV and fall asleep in front of it for hours. A piping hot turkey has been consumed. Roast potatoes. Vegetables including the much-loathed Brussels sprout. The odd bacon rasher rolled up over a sausage. Wine. Beer. Xmas pudding as dessert. It all leads to us opening our belts and letting out trapped wind.

Swedish Christmas consists of a Christmas ham, potatoes, cold slices salmon, pickled herring, salad, and…hold on, wasn't this the same food that was served at Midsummer wasn't it? Plus isn't some of it supposed to be warm? Have I missed something here? Then I found out that some of it is warm including meatballs, small sausages, porridge, the unavoidable sprouts, something called Janssons frestelse, ribs and lutfisk. Lutfisk is a piece of fish that has been prepared with lye and looks like normal white fish. It's not. It actually has a jelly like texture with the slight taste of rubber. Yet another seafood dish with an acquired taste. Don't get me wrong. I like the Christmas food. It tastes great but I am used to a meal that's 100% warm. In the UK, we even set fire to our dessert. When you think about it, you would have thought that a country that experiences serious minus temperatures in the winter would jump at the chance to cook a really hot meal and set fire to some of it, but for some reason, it doesn't happen. This is where the arguments can start and I will simply say that it's a case of what you are used to. Sweden is used to their Christmas food and think that the English Christmas dinner is bland whereas the English are used to their Christmas dinner and think that Swedish Christmas dinner is, well, for want of a better expression, mostly cold.

COLD FOOD

It's not just the food that is halfway to being cold. It's the plates too. I don't know if my home in England was like anybody else's, but my mother always warmed up the dinner plates in an oven that was cooling down, just to keep the food you are eating as warm as it can be. Sometimes, she would go too far and the plates would feel as if they had come freshly out of a kiln, burning through your dinner tray, through your clothes and to the skin of your legs. You see, long gone are the days that many English families would sit around the dining table, conversing about different things. These days, many dining tables stand dormant in testament to how things used to be in olden times with people much preferring trays that they can balance on their laps, awaiting a dinner in front the TV. Even *the Simpsons* use a dining table. The Swedes, as do must of Europe, do the exact opposite. Most families, if not all, will use that expensive dining table they bought, gathering their loved ones around it and will make the effort to lay the table with serviettes. Nobody's lap will be scolded around Swedish dinnertime and the use of plastic trays is something that will shock and confuse most of them. For me, cold plates are not something I'm used to, and it makes me scoff down my food before it gets cold.

DESSERTS

If the mostly cold food hasn't warmed you to Sweden then maybe the desserts will. England may well have puddings galore with some you can set fire to, but the Swedes can't get enough of ice cream. The facts state that Sweden is the country that guzzles down the most ice cream per year, beating the UK and even the USA. It's bizarre that a country that can suffer from minus temperatures for many a winter month would indulge in something that makes them colder. I remember shivering down the road towards the tube stop, wrapped up in a woolly hat, scarf and gloves plus a thick cardigan and hearing some distant xylophone-esque tones. I shook my head and concentrated on getting to my tube stop for some kind of indoor warmth when I heard it again. I wasn't mistaken. It was an ice cream van. An ice cream van that was doing the rounds in the middle of December. -20 degrees Celsius. I don't know how an ice cream business would justify trying to sell anything when it's -20, but it appears that they must still be able to do it regardless of people turning into ice cubes. And how does a Swede justify buying an ice cream in this situation? Do they say to themselves:

- It's -20 and I'm freezing but I'll gladly lower my core temperature for the sake of eating an ice cream.

It struck me that the Swedes have an addiction

and a lot of understanding is needed when you see somebody eating an ice-lolly in these conditions but it does explain the statistics.

Ice creams are thrown to the side and left to melt come February when the popular *semla* plops its way onto the shelves of cafés everywhere. Most Swedes will shell out and invest in a few *semla*s over the weeks that they are available and most businesses will also make time for a *semla*-break during a working day. A *semla* is basically a doughnut gone wrong with some-body somewhere deciding that they would cut the top off it and fill it with whipped cream and almond paste instead of having a jammy middle.

As you bite down into a *semla*, you may encounter the first problem of the cream squirting out from the sides and running down your fingers. After you have removed the top, the biggest trap that anyone will fall into is to use it to scoop up the cream and paste, leaving you with the second problem of hav-ing the fairly bland doughnutty base to chew through. The third problem that I have with the *semla* is that it really doesn't taste nice and feels as if my arter-ies are being severely clogged. Of course, this is just my opinion and as an outsider, I don't think Swedes would expect any foreigners to like it, and although some do, most Swedish faces light up when it's *semla* season.

The Swedes also like to do odd things to confec-tionary. I was always excited as a young boy when my

119

dad would nip down to the local shop on a Sunday morning to buy a newspaper. A packet of milk gums was my weapon of choice. They were white, chewy, creamy and sickly sweet. Not quite as sickly sweet as a Cadbury's cream egg but it was a close. Sweden also has sickly sweet confectionary but it also has something else. Salty liquorice. I got the shock of my life when I popped a chunk of the black candy in my mouth as I had expected the white powder coating to be sugar. If the exploding cans of seafood don't get you, and the *semla* has avoided blocking your arteries, this sneaky chunk of camouflaged candy will trick you out.

FAST FOOD

What do Swedes do when they fancy a quick bite to eat? A nibble to fill that empty stomach void that sounds like thunder? Easy. They go and buy a korv med bröd that is largely sold anywhere you seem to turn. There's really nothing much to talk about here in terms of food. You get a bite to eat and probably also nothing nutritious to boot, but what I want to talk about here is the actual korv med bröd phrasing. If you translate this into English it actually means sausage with bread, which does what it says on the tin. The Swedes didn't opt for hot dog as this might sound strange to them and the more you think about it, it should sound strange to native English speakers too. Is a hot dog made out of real dog? It's hard to tell sometimes but I'm of the persuasion and common human decency that it's not. If the Swedes did call their sausage with bread a hot dog then it would translate to varm hund which would just mean warm dog and that's hardly appetising to anybody.

DRINK

When it comes to looking for a beer to wash down your sausage with bread, then you'll encounter something called a stor stark, which translated means big strong. Many bars and restaurants and even cafés will have a special offer on a big strong and it is supposed to lure punters into their bar. If you are lucky, you might be served up a simple lager, and although there is nothing wrong with that, it's a standard lager that just does the job. If you are unlucky, then you'll be served up a Swedish lager instead, a beer glass full of something that tastes seemingly like combined chemicals that have been brought together in an attempt to make it taste nice. The makers of the lagers have obviously taste-tested their own lager and added just enough alcohol to try and disguise the taste of it and failed miserably. It's the only lager I have tried that actually gives you a hangover as you are drinking it, a feat that no other lager can claim. There

121

are some commercial Swedish beers and lagers that do taste good but you'll just have to try each one and find one you like. If someone offers you a stor stark, it's best to eye it with suspicion. If in doubt, and you really want to try something Swedish, go for the microbreweries instead, just to be on the safe side.

The one thing Brits notice straight away is the size of the stor stark. It falls 168ml short of the English pint and will leave some Brits complaining that they'll have to spend more to get plastered. I think the reason for the 400ml glass is to compensate for the stor stark being nasty and causing you to get drunk quicker than you usually would with a quality 568ml English beer or ale. This won't stop some from complaining and if it really makes so much of a difference, you'll find some English pubs somewhere in the bigger cities that do serve up proper UK pints.

If you want to drink at home, your usual ritual of going to the off-licence, at any hour of the day, to pick up a six-pack or bottle of wine will become a thing of the past. The supermarkets are only allowed to sell alcoholic drinks up to 3.5% proof so if you have just moved to Sweden, you'll quickly be disappointed if you wanted drinks with oomph for your now almost alcohol free party. The government in Sweden keeps a watchful eye on alcohol as they, apparently, believe that everybody is going to be irresponsible in some way if they made everything available like the UK does. To be able to keep their beady eye on the drinking situation, they came up with *Systembolaget*, a government-run supermarket that sells alcohol above 3.5% proof. It's a slightly strange concept because an alcoholic will still be able to give in to their vice when *Systembolaget* opens and only serve to limit the hours of availability for every other customer. So, once you know when your local *Systembolaget* opens and shuts, you'll just have to memorise it, otherwise it's weak beers for you my friends.

It's my personal choice and opinion that when I want to drink something, be it beer or something stronger, I would rather pay a bit extra for the sheer fact that I'll be getting a drink worthy of my taste buds. Brits will complain until they are blue in the face about beer prices in Sweden being hugely inflated compared to England but that's what you get when you move here. Unless you're willing to subject your tongue to the dubious taste of a stor stark, and suffer from an instant hangover, you won't find anything that's of quality at that price. There was one time when I went to an afterwork. An afterwork is where restaurants and pubs will lay on free food to go with your drinks ordered from 4 p.m. to around 8 p.m. on Fridays. Free food? The likelihood of this happening in the UK would be non-existent, but it doesn't stop me turning up with countless Swedes on a Friday evening to guzzle down beer and chomp on chicken drumsticks. Although some people will stay out for a while most will take advantage of this offer and substitute their dinner for it, subsequently leaving after the food dries up or out.

When I turned up at a connoisseur pub in the middle of Stockholm, I was shocked to see some of the beer prices going over 100 kronor. Although feeling slightly faint, I ordered a MAD beer, which was based on the comic, and was warned that it would cost 120 kronor. I just shrugged my shoulders and was really curious to find out what an expensive 120 kronor beer would taste like. As the bartender wiped away the excess and served me a perfect pint of liquid nectar, friends watched in horror as I handed over 120 kronor.

"Are you kidding? You paid 120 kronor for a beer?" they asked as the cold, malty drink satisfied my tongue. It was certainly something to behold as I answered, "Yes. Yes I did just pay 120 kronor for this".

It wasn't something I wanted to share with people, but I let very close friends take a quick sip, measuring the amount of time from when their lips first hit the brim of the glass. The beer itself was almost undrinkable and not because it tasted bad. Quite the reverse. It tasted great. The only problem with it was that it was thick. Really thick. Thicker than a brick wall. I had only heard tall tales of Guinness being eaten rather than drunk but this was exactly the way this beer was. I didn't have to try to make it last all night, as it was too thick to drink in large gulps. If I had tried to drink at my usual pace, I would have ended up choking and being taken to hospital and I didn't want my death certificate to read: cause of death: MAD beer.

There was another time when a group of us went to another connoisseur bar, and as it was a special occasion, we decided to mark it by ordering a 1969 Prince Charles beer, much to the shock of the waiter.

"You want to drink it?" asked the waiter.

I checked the drinks menu again to check that the 1969 beer didn't come with a side order of fries or anything else. It was a drink and therefore drinkable as far I was concerned. Would I have to eat it or do something special with it?

"Yes. Of course," I answered.

The waiter looked at all of us in shock and I detected that he was slightly shaking. When he came back, he asked us once again if we wanted him to open it. We all looked at each other, confused but nodded in an approving away. He shook his head, primed the bottle opener and flipped open the bottle whilst the cap bounced onto the table.

"Do you mind if I could try it please?" asked the waiter and produced a glass from behind his back.

This was curious behaviour from a waiter, and we started to assume that we had just opened the holy grail of beers. We had probably ruined his day and robbed him of his treasure as we poured a sip into his glass. He savoured the sip on his tongue and looked as if he did not want to swallow for at least a minute. The waiter finally finished his mouth-washing motion and sent the sip on its way to his bladder. It was money well spent, in my opinion, and it did taste pretty sublime although I wondered what all the bits floating around in it were. The waiter, on the other hand, went behind the bar and rang the Samaritans.

THINGS YOU HAVE LEARNT FROM THIS CHAPTER

- Bears are not served up as part of a normal Swedish dinner.

- Caffeine is your friend.

- Tubed caviar will make you shiver.

- Tubed banana caviar will make you convulse.

- Egyptians have got nothing on building pyramids out of shrimp carcasses.

- Rubik has his cube. Sweden has the crayfish.

- Highly pressured cans of manky seafood can be opened and eaten.

- Swedish Christmas dinner can be served cold or mostly cold.

- Experiencing -20 in Sweden? Pff. Go and eat ice

cream.

- A varm hund should not be eaten.

- Did you spill my pint? No, Swedish beers are just smaller.

- Some beers are just for show.

8. SHOPPING

On a normal day, on a normal street, in a normal city, there is a queue of people spanning back to the traffic lights, around the corner and back into the tube station. If you are on your way to work, you may pass such a queue like this and wonder what it is, what has happened or what can be so important that people are queuing up. Metal barriers with tape zigzagging their way into a building must mean that something of importance is happening or about to happen.

SALE!

When people realise that H&M is having a sale, people are already queuing at 7 a.m. when the store doesn't open until 10 a.m.. This means that some of these would-be customers have been queuing up for quite some time. People right in the front, in the prime positions, have sleeping bags on the ground accompanied by flasks of what I can only assume is coffee to keep them alert. Guards are employed to keep this peaceful, bargain-loving section of the public in order, making sure there are no line jumpers or pushers-in. Assuming that these people must have been queuing all night long, passers-by must think it must be a new night club opening or a new shop being opened by the Queen to attract this sort of line. No. It's just an H&M sale and a prime example of what happens when a shop advertises a SALE with the word CLEARANCE. When a SALE is advertised, Swedes seem to be injected with extra energy and behaviours that can be compared to crazy USA sales. For example, a clearance for a music store had people queuing long before the sale actually started, and by the time I had reached it, the queue was down the road, around the corner and backing out onto the tube station platform. It almost feels as if the Swedes have eaten an early breakfast just to mark the occasion of saving a few kronor at a SALE.

Are the Swedes really that desperate to queue a day in advance to save a few kronor? Are the prices that high to justify doing it? These questions can be answered, especially by the English, by judging prices on the cost of a simple beer. Yes. If the price of beer is anything to go on, it's expensive in Sweden. Even though I have lived here for ten years, I still do a mental currency conversion when I'm shopping, just to jolt the grey matter into thinking that I could probably find it cheaper online or on my next trip back home.

PRICE HUNTING

Finding the best price for a non-sale item on your wish list comes with a lot of responsibility and research. It really does pay to shop around, as there can be one hell of a price gap between the cheapest and most expensive price for your future purchase. So much of a price gap that it can sometimes run into a difference of thousands of kronor. So what does the normal mortal human do in such times of shopping crisis? You could use a price comparison website. You could choose the first shop at the top of the list with the cheapest price. You could buy that item that you've always wanted at that price only to find that you've got an email through from another shop that's not on the price comparison site. That shop is selling the item 500 kronor less than you just bought it for. 500 kronor that they didn't pay the price comparison website.

Yes, it can be annoying trying to find the best price for an item and the only real way of finding it is to go to each individual shop's website, check the prices, cross-reference this with what you have found on the price comparison site and go for it. As I said, it comes with much responsibility with the words tedious and anal springing to mind.

POSTAGE

If Ebay has come up trumps for you, and there are countless times it has for me, you'll be aware that the cost of sending something to Sweden can be astronomical. Back in the UK, just before I moved, I decided to send a surprise gift to somebody in Sweden. I had bought my items, wrapped them up carefully with great love and attention to detail. I plopped in the bubble wrap and polystyrene chips to protect against rough posty handling and made my way to the post office, humming a happy tune of contentedness. I didn't think about the fact that the parcel weighed 3kg or about the fact that it was being sent to Sweden, I just wanted to send a special something to brighten up somebody's day. You can imagine my shock when the posty clerk came back with:

"That'll be 31 pounds sterling please."

A sudden sense of confusion filled my head. Thirty-one pounds had not yet hit the receptors that triggered common sense, so I started to think of my tongue licking all of those stamps.

Boy, I sure would need to drink some water after this. Maybe I should use a sponge and a bowl of water instead of my tongue, I thought to myself, as the expensive thirty-one pounds came back to infect my common sense. Grabbing my package back, I smiled at the posty clerk and said,

"I'll come back later thanks."

I unpacked my professionally packed present and lifted out two of the items and repackaged them with the same care and attention that I had packed them with the first time around. I went back to the post office and sent it off, although it was still expensive. When my recipients received the package, they contacted me, thanking me for the present, and wondered why I had sent them something that is sold in Sweden anyway. It was after this that I promised myself that I would avoid sending parcels in or out of Sweden as often as possible.

LOYALTY CARDS AND GOLD

Penny-pinching tactics come in all shapes and sizes and nothing is more appealing than the rectangular store cards that are dished out when you visit a shop for the first time. A 20% discount off your first purchase when you sign up for a store card is all it takes for you to sign your name on an agreement sometimes and why not? It's a saving with the downside being that you will have yet another store card slipping its way into your wallet. I would need a wallet the size of a house brick if I were to leave home with every single store card collected in my time in Sweden. Don't leave home without them? Erm, yes, I think I will unless they start making coat pockets the size of Russia.

The UK has an abundance of credit card and loan adverts that will keep on pounding you relentlessly unless you give in or have been quick enough in pressing the mute button. If TV isn't bad enough, you will also be inundated by countless credit card and loan adverts plopping their way through your letterbox on a daily basis. I possessed three credit cards and two loans in the UK and was on the slippery slope of debt, joining countless others in the UK who had done the same thing.

Credit card and loan commercials do not happen as frequently as they do in Sweden when compared, but there was a time when recycling gold for cash adverts were shown. It made me wonder if their market research had shown that people were sitting on pots of gold at home, and wanted to send it through the post to be paid a pittance. Through the post. You read that right. Now, I'm not going to suggest that every posty out there is dishonest, but when it comes to a bulky envelope with posty gold written on it, you might as well write the address down as:

Posty Gold

Robin T. Leaf

2 Half Inch Lane

Postman's Pocket

Thiefton, R0B Y0U

If you want to avoid postal charges then the good old trusty high street won't let you down, right? It all depends on if you find the shop actually open or not. Sit back and let your brain absorb a woeful tale of when I went shopping for the first time in Gothenburg.

OPENING AND CLOSING TIMES

I remember waking up at a fairly reasonable time one day. I decided to venture out into the city and check out the music stores, of which there were many. I quickly found out that some shops didn't open until 10 a.m., so I set off at 9.30 with a view of walking through the front door just after they had opened. Imagine my shock when I reached the shop and re-alised that it was dimly lit with no signs of life within. It only meant one thing. They were shut. I knew Go-thenburg was laid back but this was ridiculous. Open at 11 a.m.? What business in the UK would possibly open at this time and shut at 6 p.m.? Slightly peeved, I wasted an hour of my life wandering around, window-shopping, and waited until the shop staff turned up to actually do some business.

Strange opening hours are not just confined to weekdays. No. Imagine it is the weekend and you want to do some furniture or electrical goods shop-ping for example. You would expect the shops to be open longer at the weekend, wouldn't you? After all, most people aren't working and have the time to shop…but no! An electrical shop that I visited on a Saturday closed at 3 p.m., and I hadn't really thought of the concept that they would close that early. I left my flat and merely plodded along, without a care in the world, expecting the shop to open until at least 6 p.m. or maybe longer. No rush. When I reached the shop, I knew I was in trouble. The shop guards were pulling the shutters over the entrance, leaving a small window of light seeping in through the front door. My watch said 2.50 p.m. but the shop staff obviously looked at their watches and read:

- We want the weekend off too, so we're closing now.

So let me get this straight, Sweden. Shops open on the weekdays at 10 a.m. and shut at 6 p.m., when people are working and will have trouble shopping after their working day is done. Then, at the weekends, when people do have the time to shop, you decide to shut early. Hmm.

Now, if you are thinking that shutting early at the weekends is a bit off, that's nothing compared to when school holidays come around. Smaller shops and restaurants will actually close for weeks, maybe even months. That fancy restaurant that you visited and harped on about is now going to embarrass you as you bring your pumped up, expectant friends to its blacked out, closed door. A sign stuck to the window

136

might read "gone fishing", "closed for the holiday" or my personal favourite, "shouldn't you be on holiday too?" Yes, bizarre as it sounds, when business owners decide to go on holiday, they just go on holiday, leaving their premises more closed than the way into Australia when customs have discovered you are carrying fruit about your person. Shops in the UK would never close just for owners to go on holiday, opting instead to bring in substitute staff, usually friends or students, to cover.

ID

Once you actually do get into a shop when it's open, there's nothing really out of the ordinary that will surprise you. That is until you reach the cashier and are asked the question:

- Leg?

- Leg? you might reply, You want to see my leg? Which one?

- Leg-itee-ma-s-hoon.

- Legit i-ma-what?

- Du måste visa leg! Erm. Legitimate?

- You're asking me if I am legitimate or not? That's a bit personal isn't it?

137

At this point, after having shown the cashier both your legs, and having been asked if you are legitimate or not, you'll probably be scratching your head in bewilderment when you are not being allowed to buy something. What the cashier is actually asking for is ID and you can do that through an ID card, driving licence, or passport. Once you have handed over your ID, it is then either looked at and returned or scanned by some shops. Even if you have bought the simplest of items, you could be asked for your card to be scanned. I often believe that big brother is watching and at any moment crack SAS squads will burst through the roof, take me down and arrest me for buying a birthday card.

ONE-WAY SYSTEMS

The biggest trap, almost literally, is the one-way system that you have to abide by in certain shops. As soon as you walk through their front door, you know that you have no choice but to follow the arrows they have painted neatly on the ground in front of you. The way you came in has now been shut behind you leaving you feeling like Indiana Jones with the sinking feeling that a large boulder might be on its way to crush you. There is almost no way out. If you are like me then you will only have a time limit of thirty minutes to find the exit before the mind numbing store music, one-way system and large, suspended sale placards mash your brain into pulp. Sometimes, it is hopeless. Some of these stores are so large that you can't help but get stuck or lost, and after those thirty minutes has run out, you'll start forgetting what it is you went in there for in the first place. You'll probably end up at the checkout with a picture frame, a plastic kitchen implement and the in-store pencil that is so blunt, you'll have to buy a sharpener as well to be able to use it.

HOME SHOPPING AND THE FAKTURA

If shops being closed, showing your leg, getting stuck in a one-way system or having the possibility of being profiled by big brother has put you off high street shopping, then you can always try the trusty net or home shopping to satisfy your shopping needs. There are a multitude of clothes shops that operate out of the town Borås that send catalogues out for every season. Although, judging by the amount you receive, it feels more like every week. When I first settled into my new surroundings in 2003, I took the opportunity to flick through a home shopping catalogue to check if there was anything different the Swedes do compared to the UK.

- MP3 players, headphones, cables, - nothing wrong so far, as I continued flicking through the pages, - games consoles, dildos, TVs...hold on... dildos?

Having the same reaction to seeing a ghost, I quickly flicked back the pages and there they were. I wasn't imagining it. Dildos. Lots of them. Some large. Some small. Some colourful. Others that looked as if they could inflict pain. My shock wasn't due to what they were but mostly to do with the fact that they were in full plain view, for everyone to see, in a normal, harmless looking home shopping catalogue. I couldn't imagine Littlewoods selling dildos at any point in the future as these kinds of things are usually swept under the carpet in England. Well, maybe not swept literally under the carpet, more swept into a shoebox and hidden out of the reach of any potential dildo hunter.

Ordering from home shopping catalogues or the net is nothing out of the ordinary but the way you pay for things is. There are a few options to choose from compared to the UK where it's a case of pay up now and we'll send your item. In Sweden, you can also pay up front or have the item sent first and a bill sent later, called a *faktura*. The trick to the *faktura* is remembering to pay it. It sounds like an obvious thing to point out, but if you have been used to paying for everything up front, the *faktura* can just be cast aside and be buried under those clothing and home shopping catalogues I mentioned earlier. A month later, you'll get the shock of your life when

you are sent the same *faktura* again with charges added to it for not paying. As if things weren't expensive
already.

FOOD SHOPPING

Now we come to a part of everyone's life whether
you like shopping or not. Food shopping. It's a chore
we all have to do because we all have to eat unless
your name is David Blaine doing a stupid stunt in a
box somewhere. Back in good ol' Blighty, the tactics
are simple. You grab a trolley, you dash around with
a set list, scoop everything you want into the trolley, checkout within thirty minutes if you can and go
home to unpack. It was always the way that it was
approached when shopping with my dad. My mum
always had the intentions of dashing but couldn't
resist squeezing fruit. This is a big no-no in speed
shopping as it will harm your chances of getting out
of Dodge within thirty minutes, increasing the risk
of brain pulping.

Squeezing fruit may slow you down more than
a snail slithering out of a UK post box, but Swedes
take part in a ritual that will hold you up more at the
checkout. This is called barcode assembly. The days
are gone where the UK days of slinging your would-
be purchases willy-nilly on the conveyor belt, making the cashier work hard for their pay. In Sweden,

your shopping has to be arranged in a neat single file on the conveyor belt with the bar codes facing you. Once all your items are out of your basket and on the conveyor belt, the cashier will thank you for not giving them repetitive strain injury. They won't have to move a muscle or struggle to find those bar codes to scan. Immigrants from the UK look in wonder at this phenomenon in supermarket etiquette and wonder what it is all about. In the UK, food shopping is hurled onto the conveyor belt without any particular finesse. Wallop. Here you go cashier. Start doing your plinging.

CHRISTMAS MARKETS

There are no such hold ups when it comes to Christmas markets, the time of year when you wander round, looking at handicrafts and eating roasted almonds. There are no barcodes in sight. Nobody with conveyor belts. No cashiers who are at risk from repetitive strain injury. The deal with Christmas markets is to pick up special items as presents for others or for yourself, in a nice relaxed atmosphere. There's nothing that could possibly ruin this time of happiness and calm. That is until you reach a trader selling reindeer meat at Liseberg in Gothenburg. To tempt you, traders will lay on free samples of their wares in the hope you'll come away with a piece of them. The reindeer meat trader was no exception.

"Yes. You can try. You can try. It's lovely meat if you haven't tried it," said the market trader, pointing to a tray of diced reindeer meat.

I picked up a few cubes and was about to eat them when something caught the corner of my eye. A reindeer. Thanks to the animal exhibition, the reindeer had been placed directly behind the trader with one, curious, sad looking reindeer standing behind him. I looked at my cubes of meat and then at the reindeer. I could swear that it squinted at me and tilted its head in a don't-eat-me way.

"Try it! Try it!" urged the market trader.

I looked at the reindeer cubes again. Then at the trader. Then at the reindeer. I couldn't do it. Placing the cubes back down on the plate, I turned to the trader and remarked, pointing:

"I can't eat it. I could be eating one of his or her relatives!"

As I pointed to the literally doe-eyed reindeer, the trader turned around and looked at the animal exhibit-turned-protest. Looking slightly scared, the reindeer retreated back to its comrades, having achieved its mission in putting me off eating its sibling.

THINGS YOU HAVE LEARNT FROM THIS CHAPTER

- Bears can't be bought at a supermarket.

- Sales turn Swedes into masters of queuing.

- Shopping around can mean the difference between paying Oxfam or Harrods prices.

- Postage stamps can be more expensive than the item you are posting.

- Sending gold through the post does not make up for the last point.

- Opening hours should be renamed shutting hours.

- Showing your legs will not make shopping easier.

- Cashiers have feelings too.

- A reindeer is not just for Christmas. It's for Christmas markets.

9. HOUSING & LIVING

One problem that many immigrants will probably come across is where to live. A minefield of new terms will have to be learnt and negotiated, the prospect of moving every six months if you are renting in the larger cities will be painful and buying a property could potentially cause cardiac arrest. Yes. It can be tricky living in Sweden.

BUYING A PROPERTY

In Sweden, you are unlikely to see any estate agents' 'for sale' boards nailed up, cluttering up the area and making things look untidy. Instead, you're more likely to see a small sandwich board standing outside a property with an arrow pointing to it or small posters stuck to its windows. It's not the hard sell that the UK is used to with multiple agents fighting over one property.

How do you go about buying a property? Although newspaper adverts are still used, the net is the way to go to check on the sales market. Once you spot the house or apartment of your dreams, it's on to the estate agent to organise a viewing. After this, it's onto the final important part of buying it. Whilst the UK opts to put out expensive prices to be bartered down, Sweden uses a bidding system, a little bit like Ebay but with houses and flats instead. It's here that most Swedes will have that cardiac arrest as they wonder if their bid will be the one that gets them the property of their dreams. So the prices you see in the papers or online are not necessarily the price you will pay for it unless there is a fixed price.

PRICES & CHARGES

Prices for properties on the other hand are something to be savoured. When I first learnt that a flat outside of Gothenburg was selling for the equivalent of £18,000 (circa 2004), I was flabbergasted. £18,000? I couldn't have bought a mid-terrace cardboard box for that price in the UK. When I researched prices more, I realised that the further out in the sticks a property was, the cheaper it was. Crazily cheap. The only properties that were expensive were situated on a coastline somewhere with a view of the sea or in cities. At these prices, I felt that I should buy a whole village as an investment and call it 'Linterby'.

If you are the proud owner of a flat then there is something you should know, especially if you are like me and moved from the UK. On top of your mortgage, you have to pay a monthly fee to the housing association called *bostadsrätt* for the general upkeep of the building, the surrounding area and rubbish collecting.

RENTING

Maybe you don't want to buy your own pad. Maybe you want to rent a place and not be tied down to anything. Maybe you just want to drift for a while. It's ok. You can do it in Sweden but in the big cities, don't expect to live anywhere longer than six months unless you are lucky. The rental market depends mostly on people who have decided to go on holiday or a sabbatical and want to rent out their properties. When the owners come back to claim their property, it will be you that has to move on and find somewhere else to live. If you are not worried about your furniture being large heavy cardboard boxes for all of eternity, until you find a place that lets you settle for more than six months, then this is the solution for you. The other alternative to this is to put your name on a waiting list for a first hand contract but be prepared to wait until the Earth stops revolving to get one of those.

SUPPOSED SLUM & GARDENS

The first flat that I moved into was described as being in a slum area of Gothenburg but I think somebody somewhere had not seen some of the slums in the UK or USA before labelling it. I had never before come across a slum abode that had a small gym, sauna, recycling house, basement and loft space that I could use any time.

Although the flat didn't come with a garden, the block was built in the midst of a forest, which, to all intents and purposes, became the back garden. The Swedes have the attitude that open land and countryside is considered nature, so erecting high fences and cordoning off a small section, as the UK does, wouldn't be aesthetically pleasing. So sometimes, a garden is generally the natural countryside that surrounds your house or flat no matter where you live. If someone chooses to walk past your house, through that same countryside, the right of way is given to that person.

KEEPING YOUR PAD TIDY & THE RULES

Once you have bought a place to live, several things happen. Decorating is to be expected as usual. Buying furniture. Buying kitchen utensils. All fairly nor-

mal. Once you start inviting people over or expect
someone to show up, this is where things really happen. A huge clean-up operation has to take place
whether or not your house or flat looked tidy as it
was. This isn't simply a case of brushing things under the nearest sofa or bed; this is getting the flat
ready as if you are going to sell it tomorrow. The
floor has to be spotless. The sideboards must not
have a speck of dust on them and the same goes for
the TV. There shouldn't be a burnt out light bulb to
be found in any socket of any room. Most importantly, you should make sure you stock up the food
cupboards and fridge. It takes some effort to do all
of the above and by the time you have done it all,
your guests might have rung and cancelled on you,
but at least you have got a clean flat or house out of
it.

If you are expecting guests from another country
to grace your house or flat with their presence, then
certain rules exist and have to be drawn up, much
in the same way the ten commandments were. One
of these rules is 'thou shalt not draw the curtains'.
Curtains in a Swedish flat or house are for decorative
uses only and are not to be used as nature intended.
A Swede will be mortally horrified if a foreign guest
tries to draw the curtains and might quickly shout at
them to stop, leaving the guest looking confused as
to what they have done wrong.

Swedish windows are decorated for the people

outside in the same way a shop window is dressed. You see, the curtains that you couldn't pull were not only decorations for the inside; they are decorations for the outside world. The main questions for me when I saw this was:

- Will people see my bum when I am getting dressed?

- Aren't you scared of burglars seeing what you have and breaking in?

The first question's answer was less then complimentary: Your bum is really not that special. The second question, however, was easily answered. Front doors open in the opposite direction compared to the UK, so if a burglar did try to break in, they can't kick the door in.

If a burglar did manage to break into a flat, I wondered if they would have to take their shoes off before clearing away all the valuables. It's another rule of entering a Swedish home. 'Thou must take off all forms of footwear and leave them at the front door'. In England, this has never been the case, as we believe the carpets will take care of any offending dirt that may scrape or fall off onto it. After all, if you can't see it then surely it can't exist.

Playing into the hands of this rule is the tiptoe tactic when someone has just cleaned a floor. If you can't be bothered to take off your shoes and want to fetch something across the room, you just tiptoe

150

across because that surely means that your feet aren't actually making contact with the floor and, therefore, not making it dirty again. It's something that all of us have done at some point in time and it's something that most accept as well for some bizarre reason. It's preferred, in Sweden, to use the shoes off method at all times, which can be a bit irritating if you have to come and go from your house or flat. For example, if you have just come back from emptying the various bags or bins of rubbish, you'll have taken your shoes off countless times. Now I know why Swedes used to wear clogs. It's at this point where you might want to wash your hands too, which brings me to my next subject: the bathroom.

THE BATHROOM

There are many rumours of bathrooms and toilets being different in European countries. For example, a toilet that I encountered in Amsterdam had a ledge underneath where you sat down with the bowl taking the remaining space. I'm not sure why you would want to take a crap on a ledge, look at it and then flush it away, but I suppose there has to be a reason for it. The only reason I could think of would be the recent trend in health shows that detect how healthy you are by looking at your poo. In Japan, they invented a toilet that can analyse your poo and give you a detailed report on your health afterwards. If my parent's habits were anything to judge, this toilet would have had a really strange report when they flushed the contents of the kitty litter down it.

- You should cut down on eating grit, grass and insects, and you seem to have an unhealthy addiction to cat food.

Anyway, in Sweden, there is no such poo ledge like Amsterdam and they certainly don't have a toilet that talks to you. However, they do have two types of flush, which have to be briefly explained if you have friends or family visiting for the first time:

- 1 is for wee and 2 is for poo.

- Oh right. I see.

The two-flush system is a good idea and saves on water, but one thing in the bathroom that hits the spot is the shower. Power showers with pressure and a proper mixer. Choose your degree of warm or cold, turn on the tap and go crazy. It's a whole new world of showering in Sweden compared to the UK.

For those who have not experienced showering in the UK, then let me explain. England still has the hot and cold tap system where many have bought the rubber or plastic shower attachment that you fit to the taps. This has a fatal flaw for not being able to mix water to the temperature that you want before it hits your skin. For example, if I think about my parent's bathroom, the taps should be re-titled ice

152

for cold and lava for hot. That's not even an exaggeration. You could make a cup of tea directly from the hot tap and freeze peas with the cold tap. Upon fitting the shower implement to the taps, you encounter a problem. For anyone who plans to take a shower in the UK, here is my guide to getting the temperature right:

GUIDE TO HOW TO GET THE RIGHT TEMPERATURE WATER FOR A SHOWER IN THE UK AND WHAT TO DO IF IT GOES WRONG.

• The first tip is to make sure that the proposed shower tubes are connected to the taps tightly. You don't want either one coming off when you have the taps on at a rapid speed, as this will give you either the ice or lava mentioned above. Once secured, you can start mixing.

• The mixing is a long and arduous process in which many people have lost some skin, gone to casualty or in extreme cases, not washed at all. Turn on the cold tap first. It should be a steady rate but not too fast.

• Now, turn on the hot tap – SLOWLY! Don't over

do it. A slip of the hand and you'll need skin grafts.

• Still cold? It usually is at this stage. Keep nudging the hot tap really slowly. So slowly that'll you'll think the evening has come round quickly or that you have died.

• Just burnt yourself? This can happen. The slight nudge that you just did was a nudge too far. You'll have to go back to step 2 now.

• The best thing to do now is to imagine that you are cracking a safe. Remember those small nudges you were doing before? Make them half the size. This will do the trick.

• Got the right temperature? Well done. You've cracked it. Now relax and take a 'shower' but be on your guard. If someone uses the taps down stairs or somewhere else in the same building, then start ringing casualty.

Thankfully, there is no safe cracking to be done in a Swedish bathroom and all apartments and homes that I have been to have the proper mixers. Now that I have moved over to power showers that work prop-

154

erly, I really can't understand the attitude of people who want two separate taps. Some may call it quaint and stylish. I call it impractical and you end up wasting a lot of water trying to get the temperature right. These days, when I visit England, I just fill the tub with water and be done with it. I'm not wasting my mornings using the safe cracking method anymore.

WINDOWS

If you are lucky enough to live in a new apartment, you'll find that all the windows are triple glazed and if you are unlucky to live somewhere slightly older, you might have double-glazing instead. It's a far cry from the drafty single glazing that I became accustomed to when I was a young lad, trying hard to grow up and not die of pneumonia. The Swedes may like to go skiing or eat ice cream when it's -20 outside and jump in icy lakes, but they can't tolerate a cold flat or house. This is why they position all radiators under the windows, which is the unwritten rule that nobody told the builders of my parent's house about, and they install triple glazing as standard. In England, double-glazing is still seen as a step onto the next rung of window improvement and is still not installed as standard. For example, my parent's house was built in 1997 and still didn't come with double-glazing, making it feel a lot colder to the point where

155

I have to throw a quilt over myself when I am sitting in the living room. Of course, I have really got used to how warm homes are here in Sweden and how well insulated they are, but shouldn't this be the case in every country? As my parents shiver and freeze their way through another winter, with the boiler hanging on for dear life, and the radiators positioned in all the wrong places, I spare them a thought as I walk around my apartment in shorts and a t-shirt in the mornings where the temperature reads -20 outside.

So, to summarise, when you have had your top property bid accepted, you can move to a place where burglars can look at you through your curtainless, triple glazed windows into your toasty warm home. Most, if not all, front doors open in the other direction so don't worry about the burglar trying to break in. If he or she manages, then ask them take their shoes off at the doormat and apologise to them for not being able to tidy up the place beforehand.

THINGS YOU HAVE LEARNT FROM THIS CHAPTER

- Bears don't have to bid on a dwelling.

- Cardboard boxes can make a good alternative to furniture.

• Slums have saunas, gyms, recycling house and storage space.

• Curtains are not for pulling.

• Burglars can't break in but if they do, they must remove their shoes.

• Tiptoeing across a clean floor will not avoid it becoming dirty.

• Keep your finger on the number to the emergency services when you take a shower in the UK.

• Insulation and triple-glazing-free? Welcome to the UK and freeze.

10. SOCIETY

Are the Swedish really distant, cold people or is it just a myth? Many looking in from other countries may wonder about this stereotype but now that I have lived in Sweden for ten years, I'm here to bust that myth.

STEREOTYPES

I have met Swedes that have fulfilled the cold and distant stereotype to the letter. After just meeting someone for the first time, you would usually expect to have a conversation but for some, this is like getting blood out of a stone. It has to be said, some Swedes are very nutlike with what they want you to know about themselves, giving you the outer layer of the shell, ready at all times to take the nut away when you try to crack it open. On the other hand, I have met Swedes who want to tell you everything about themselves all in the space of one hour after meeting them. They have already cracked the nut open and they'll force feed it to you whether you like it or not. There's not a definitive answer to why this happens other than everybody is different and that's not unusual anywhere in the world.

The stand-offish behaviour stereotype is reinforced when British ex-pats seem to get annoyed when Swedes don't say please when asking for help with something. The reason for this is a simple one – there isn't really a word for please in Swedish (the word - snälla - does mean please but is only used in certain circumstances). Instead, a Swede might just say - tack, which means thanks, or more likely, nothing at all, leaving the English assuming that they are the rudest people that exist. In defence of the Swedes, you can't exactly expect someone to say please when it's a word that doesn't exist and therefore can't say it. It's the same thing when Brits hold doors open, expecting a thank you for taking time out to help them. When a thank you or please goes astray, Brits will immediately criticise Swedes for their rudeness and lack of manners.

OPEN SOCIETY

The apparent open society in which Swedes live in couldn't be more obvious when talking about Swedish celebrities. Thanks to everybody being equal, celebs can sometimes be spotted doing some shopping, drinking coffee or just generally wandering around a town or small city. If this happens to you, you might become a little star struck, point your finger and say to the person next to you,

- Isn't that….?

The person might answer - yes, it is - but you'll be too busy convincing yourself it couldn't possibly have been the celeb in question. I have been in the situation where there has been a celeb in a café and I wasn't sure whether or not I should talk to them or not. It's a huge grey area and if you did it in the UK, you might be most likely to get an - I'm busy - reply. No such thing happened here. The celeb in question was extremely friendly and after I had told him about a project I was working on, he gave me a few contacts to call. Now that's something that certainly wouldn't happen in the UK. A similar thing happened when I first moved to Gothenburg when I was working on a project for my SFI course (Svenska för invandrare). I walked into the same music shop that was shut when I tried to visit it before and asked the shop manager about bands in Gothenburg. I needed information from bands and wondered if he had any contacts that I could call or meet with a view of interviewing. He replied that it wasn't a problem at all and gave me a few phone numbers that turned out to be high profile music artists operating in Gothenburg. This was something else. It seemed as if I could just ask anybody for any information and they would dish it out. If I had asked for the direct line to The Swedish Royal Family, I might have got that too.

Even if shop owners didn't give out details of celebs and even if celebs themselves didn't dish out information, there is another certain way of getting it, and that's through the tax office called Skatteverket. Thanks to the Swedish open society, you can go into Skatteverket and request information you want on anybody. They're not even allowed to ask you what the information is for either. Now to the normal average person this is probably a surprise, but no big deal as you'll never need to do it but for the below average, mentally ill lunatic, this could be like waving a red flag in front of a bull. Sure, there are laws against stalking and harassment but it's a bit late to do anything about it after it's happened. It would certainly cut down on the amount of work a spy or hitman would have to do.

- Yes. I would like information on Mr Svensson please. I would like to post him a note along with a dog turd.

- Certainly, sir. Coming right up. Here you go. You have his address, telephone number, names of next of kin and the amount of cars he has. Anything else I can help you with?

- Do you happen to know if he wears a hat all the time or if that's something he does some of the time?

- No. We can't answer any questions about hat wearing.

BUREAUCRACY

Bureaucracy, or red tape as some like to call it, is huge in Sweden and the UK. Everywhere you go, your ID card will be called upon as many times as you go to the toilet in one day. In shops, at work, official buildings and, in pubs and clubs if you look younger than you are or are young. If you fail to have your ID card on you then you'll just have to give whoever is asking your social security number, referred to as your birth number. Swedes get them at birth, but immigrants have to apply for one through Skatteverket. Before you get your birth number, you need a residence permit. This should be fairly simple as the UK is in the EU (as of 2013), but some of my friends have not had things so easy. Some friends have had interviews with Migrationsverket (migrations office) and been asked so many questions, it felt as if they were being interrogated by secret police. One Brit changed his last name to a Swedish surname just to give himself an easier time of things. I have never been to Migrationsverket and did everything by paperwork and post, all without changing my name to Svensson or something similar.

The birth number comes in handy on your ID card. If you want an ID card, there is a simple way to do it. Swap your driving licence over to a Swedish one. If you come from the UK, there is an element of comedy in doing this.

POINTS THAT MAKE SWAPPING A UK DRIVING LICENCE FOR A SWEDISH ONE CRAZY.

Point 1

The UK drives on the left and the Swedes drive on the right.

Point 2

When it snows in the UK, the traffic grinds to a halt whereas in Sweden, it keeps rocking. This is generally due to them changing their normal tyres for winter tyres. Also, if you think beyond the fact that Swedes are more prepared for snow and ice, you would have thought the UK would have least considered the option of winter tyres but no. We will continue to be trapped in our cars on the M25 for a day or two when five millimetres of snow hits the tarmac, much to the Swedes' amusement.

Point 3

Sweden's driving test not only teaches you the best way to flatten an elk, it also teaches you to drive on ice too. A special ice rink is set up to test a potential driver's ability to cope with winter conditions. Smart, eh? If the UK had this kind of test, we wouldn't know what to do. If it is anything like handling ice on actual UK roads, we'd probably just park the car and ring the nearest relative to complain.

Point 4

Although the UK moved over to the card form of driving licence, it still couldn't let go of the old habits by making you keep a paper counter-part. A paper counterpart that is much too big for any wallet, even my house brick sized wallet. If you swap over to a Swedish licence, you can ditch that paper section. Have a ritual burning if you want to. It's done. It's gone. You don't need it anymore.

Yes. Despite driving on the other side of the road, not being able to drive in freezing conditions, and missing out on a majority of what is included in the Swedish Driving Test, a Brit is allowed to swap their licence over with minimum fuss. For my American friends, imagine how jealous they were when I told them my story while they were applying for a licence and had to take a driving test again. Ho hum. It pays to be in the European Union, I guess.

RAGGARE

Keeping on the subject of cars, a unique phenomenon happens in Sweden. Sections of Swedish society, especially in the countryside, drive around in '50's and '60's American cars. The people driving these cars are called *raggare*. Some of them have adopted an almost '50's style of dress and will drive their pristine automobiles with fins and shiny chrome wheels around with pride, through forests and out onto the main roads. In the UK, seeing an old American car would be a rare sight, but in Sweden, it's odds on that you will see quite a few if you stay any length of time. A trip to the west coast town of Lysekil was the first time I had any contact with *raggare* and it made me react:

- Wow! Look. There's an old American car.

After I spotted one American car after another, it was clear that this was the venue for some kind of *raggare* car appreciation festival as a multitude of Cadillacs and Chevys swept into town.

166

NUMMERLAPP

An effective speed bump in dealing with official organisations is the number ticket system known as the
nummerlapp. It doesn't matter who you are dealing
with, all of them will want you to grab a small coloured square of paper from a machine with a huge
arrow above it with the words - ta nummerlapp - written on it. This small coloured square of paper will be
ejected from the machine at a fairly slow speed and
will have a number on it. This is where you are in
the queue. It's similar to that tired robotic voice you
have all heard when you get put on hold when ringing an institution that you hoped would deal with
you quickly. There's no real difference between being
helped in a queue by telephone or in person. You will
always wake up especially early to be first in line and
then find that everyone else had the same idea and
end up in the middle, or worse, last. It's always been
amazing to me that a huge bunch of people got in
the line faster than you when you called at 9 a.m. on
the dot. How did the thirty-four people get the jump
on you? If you are to get anywhere in person, then
camping out like the line for the H&M sale or new
collection would serve you well.

Usually, when you first get your nummerlapp,
you will glance at your number and will be overjoyed
when it reads the number three. Great! That's right
at the start you'll say to yourself. When you look up

at the number display however, you'll quickly realise that it reads eighty-six, leaving you sixteen places behind.

Nummerlapp systems just aren't solely isolated off and confined to official entities. No. You'll find them in supermarkets to help people queue at the delicatessen counter or cheese counter, in shops to help people queue to be served, and in banks just because they like you to queue. It's a mystery to whether they speed up processes or lengthen the time you have to wait but some people get impatient and leave early. This, in turn, will make whoever is operating the number machine, hop over each missing person slowly.

Number twenty-three… wait… wait… Number twenty-four… wait… wait…

After reaching number thirty-four, it'll be clear that the day has moved so slowly that it practically gave up and went home instead. Even if you do happen to be the only person in the shop, you are still made to take a nummerlapp. It's a requirement to actually being served. No piece of square coloured paper with a number on it? Sorry, pal. Maybe it won't be long until the Swedish adopt this system for parties and have people queuing up at barbecues.

The worst time and place for the nummerlapp system is when you have to visit the doctor. If you haven't been able to book a time with a doctor, there is a drop-in system at emergency clinics. This is where you'll encounter the nummerlapp. There was one time in Gothenburg where an emergency involving a horse-fly bite made my girlfriend and I travel to the emergency ward of one of these drop-in wards. After taking a seat, I noticed the time tick slowly by, partially sleeping through a couple of hours, only to awake to find my girlfriend still waiting by the side of me. We had been waiting for four hours but it got worse. Another hour passed to the point where I thought that this could be a story for the TV show *I Shouldn't Be Alive*. After time passed into the sixth hour and the numbers ticked slowly by, we were eventually seen to and walked away with a prescription for a tube of topical cream to sooth away the bite. A bite so severe that it had ballooned my girlfriend's leg to such an extent that she had trouble walking. The time was worth wasting.

SWEDISH MIDSUMMER

Luckily, parties don't have a nummerlapp system but do have their own quirky peculiarities that make them Swedish. The absolute epitome of Swedishness is Midsummer where masses of people assemble in parks to raise a *Midsommarstång* or Midsummer pole. The idea behind it all is to celebrate the fact the much forgotten orangey thing in the sky... what was it called again?... you remember… it's hot and fiery… the sun… the fact that the sun will shine for the most hours in a day before it starts setting faster and disappears altogether for what seems way too long. While the sun's future is not thought about, Swedes everywhere will be dancing around the pole and singing traditional Midsummer songs like the one about small frogs that go kvack and pigs that go nöff. For fresh immigrants to the country, this presents a challenge. Although you'll probably feel stupid dancing around a pole and mimicking small critters that sound nothing like that in reality to ex-pats, it's something that will be forced upon you at some point. The song about small frogs is Britain's fault as it apparently comes from a French march-ing song that the Brits picked up and changed to in-sult the French by calling them frogs. One way of approaching Midsummer dancing is to throw your hands in the air, which is not part of the dance, and admit you have no idea how the dances are pulled off. You'll soon discover that the stereotype of re-served Swedes couldn't be further from the truth as you'll be holding hands with complete strangers be-fore you know it.

The Midsummer holiday is also a time where ev-erything shuts down. Remember how I mentioned restaurants and small businesses that close during this holiday? Well, this also applies to television. Of course, I'm not saying that television stations close down, I'm saying that the staff that work for them also go on holiday. Instead of displaying a screen that reads "gone fishing", morning television, known for showing the news every thirty minutes with interviews with celebs on comfy sofas in-between, will show old interviews and even large chunks of normal programs that are broadcast at other times. It left me with that *Groundhog Day* feeling that I had started a day in the same way, but thankfully I didn't take a toaster into the bathroom with me to test the theory. The closest the UK comes to this is when television staff go on strike. If this happens, films and old comedy series are shown, which many say is an improvement on the programs that are normally broadcast.

WEDDING RECEPTIONS

Wedding receptions are in a league of their own. Usually with English weddings, you would expect the father of the bride to speak, the best man, the groom's family may well say something too. Usually the speeches are fairly short and don't run over five minutes, but there are always exceptions to this rule of course. So expecting the same thing, my first wedding reception was an eye-opener to say the least. With one introduction and semi-speech out of the way, the guests all sat down with the intentions of eating the dinner. Just as my fork had pronged its way into the tender roast chicken with avocado sauce, another piece of cutlery was going to dash my chances of any digestion questions reaching my stomach.

Clink! Clink! Clink!

Yes. It was a speech. The father of the bride spoke. The speech lasted roughly ten minutes, and as my Swedish was virtually non-existent at the time, I didn't understand much of it at all. The speech was over. I quickly picked up my fork again, and reunited it with the chicken that I had intended to eat beforehand.

Clink. Clink. Clink.

This time it was the mother of the bride. As, I raised my glass at the end of this speech, I could slowly sense my stomach getting slightly agitated and growling. Soon, it would be appeased and it would get that chicken that it had been promised as I sank my fork into it again.

Clink. Clink. Clink.

This time it was the best man. This could take a while. It did. By the time this speech had finished, the steam that accompanied my meal had long gong, and the piece of chicken was now halved through my constant fork prodding. Surely, now I would be able to eat something.

Clink. Clink. Clink.

Now what? The father of the groom wanted to say

something followed by the mother. After this, the best friend of the bride also had a speech prepared. My stomach had packed up its intestines and was ready to leave by the time they had all finished speaking. As I sat down again, observing that my food was now stone cold, which was not helped by the cold plates the meal began on, I looked around with squinty accusing eyes, looking for any signs of cutlery and glass coming together to further delay quenching my hunger. I was waiting for family pets to come along to either howl or squeak next. Don't get me wrong. I don't have anything against any speeches or Swedish weddings, as they are, dare I say, more personal when compared to English weddings. They don't have any curly sandwiches or sausage rolls to spoil the day and set against the backdrop of Swedish landscapes, what more could you ask for? I just don't like lots of speeches when my stomach is complaining.

FUNERALS

Although not a time to usually celebrate, funerals are also very different. Based on my experience of English funerals, the coffin is displayed out at the front of the church on a ledge. The priest will talk for approximately thirty to forty minutes allowing other people to talk afterwards. A curtain is then drawn around the coffin automatically while the words

173

"ashes to ashes" are uttered and that is that. It's very clinical and fairly quick. Swedish funerals also have the coffin out on display, but they don't use an automatic curtain to send the deceased away. You get the chance to say goodbye to your loved one and lay some flowers on the coffin. There are no quick finalities here. There isn't a curtain that sweeps around the coffin and hides it from view. Once the funeral is over, there is the usual family mingle at the house of the deceased. For people in the UK, this will mean curly sandwiches and sausage rolls. It makes me wonder if it would have been what the deceased would have wanted. Did they write in their will:

- My belongings will be divided equally amongst my children, and I most certainly would like to have curly sandwiches and sausage rolls at the family after-funeral mingle thingy.

DON'T ASK

I made the mistake, on one of these funeral-mingling occasions, of talking to a couple that had just bought their first house. The conversation wasn't anything out of the ordinary until I asked them how much it had set them back. I could sense a small gasp of shock being let out from the people around me and deafening silence from the couple I had asked. It felt as if I had just paid them the most brutal of insults, but it turned out that, in Sweden, you are not allowed to ask somebody how much something costs, especially if it is a substantial purchase because it is considered prying into how much somebody earns. If you compare this to England, people everywhere ask how much something costs, not because they are prying, but because they just like to weigh up whether the price someone paid was a bargain or not. That's the only reason. If a price turns out to be a bargain, a Brit will say:

- Wow! You did well there.

It will leave the buyer feeling smug and satisfied that they have saved themselves money. If a price turns out to have ripped someone off, a Brit will usually just nod their head and move onto the next topic of conversation. It's now something that I try to suppress asking when talking about buying anything of any large value.

HEADSTONES

Although it is considered bad manners to ask about finances at a funeral mingle, it is, however, not considered bad manners to treat death as a natural process. So natural in fact that funeral directors have no problem in advertising headstones as if they were part of your normal grocery shopping list. Funeral director advertisements will claim that their headstones are good value for money and that they deliver and fit them all over the country. In the UK, funeral directors and headstones remain taboo until they are actually needed, and adverts in newspapers are rarely, if at all, seen. In Sweden, however, you might find yourself leaving a supermarket and questioning yourself: - I'm sure there's something I've forgotten. Bread - check. Eggs - check. Peas - check. Ah! I know - headstone!

PANT

In Swedish society, there are those little differences that make it what it is. For example, most packaged drinks, if not all of them, will have a small symbol on them with the word *pant* written underneath. The word *pant* on a bottle means that it can be recycled for money and you'll get either one or two kronor when you recycle the empty bottles or cans. Although sounding like the good idea that it is, it can lead to a couple of problems.

PANT PROBLEM ONE: KID GETS CRUSHED BY RUBBISH

When the Midsummer day rolls around, it comes with the Midsummer party where Swedes, of the mostly younger persuasion, will drink themselves under the table and onto the floor, where they will be found the following day with a hangover that makes them feel as their heads will fall off. Where drunken passed out Swedes can be found, an opportunity to make money from their demise exists, namely collecting the empty bottles and cans they left behind. Massive tidy-up operations are required after Swedish Midsummer campers have packed up and gone home, making young kids spring into action armed with large bin liners. I have to admit to having done a similar thing when I was younger after being desperate to send off for free *A View To A Kill* posters from crisp packet tokens. Crisp packets are one thing. Beer cans and bottles are another. A kid will go to great extremes to fill their large bin liner with all the *pant*-marked items so they can to get maximum profit. That's all fine and well but I saw one kid that was greatly outweighed by the sack of goodies and in danger of being crushed if he had fallen over. If he avoided being trapped by rubbish and made it to the recycling station found in most supermarkets, he would have had to have stood there for days, feeding can after can, bottle after bottle, into the machine to get the full amount of money. If you bear in mind that most of the empty cans and bottles would have been worth one krona each or more, combined with the amount of time it would have taken him to recycle everything, the risk of getting crushed by rubbish seems hardly worthwhile. Whatever floats your boat!

177

PANT PROBLEM TWO: BIN SCAVENGERS APLENTY

Another problem unique to the *pant* system comes in the shape of bin scavengers. They will rummage through any bin that happens to be in view and look for empty bottles and cans to recycle. Although it is mostly the homeless or hard up that will do this, I have seen others take to bin scavenging that you wouldn't expect to see do it.

Bin scavengers come in three species and they are as follows:

The novice

This bin scavenger does not hide from public and is not ashamed of putting both hands into the bin. This species can range from your average weirdo to a desperate person. They will usually just dive straight in, using both hands whilst talking to themselves. They will usually take a look at the bottle to make sure it is empty and if it isn't, they will gladly drink the contents to finish it off. They don't carry any type of bag, and will probably just use their trousers as a pouch to carry their offspring to the supermarket.

The amateur

The amateur bin scavenger can look like you and me. The only difference will be that they will wear market trader gloves and carry a paper shopping bag with them. They use the same technique as the novice, but with the addition of the paper bag, can collect more than your novice, making them odds on to clear up before anyone else arrives to do the same thing. I'm not sure why they would want to collect cans other than the fact that they must be very hard up for money.

The pro

The professional bin scavenger is a rare breed. They might look as if they are going to work in a shirt and tie. Don't be fooled by this cunning camouflage. The professional bin scavenger benefits from their business look and will not only use gloves, usually white ones they got from a hospital, but they will use a grabber as well. The only drawback to this method is that they collect cans very slowly, but nevertheless, the pro exists and I have seen these fellows in action a few times.

It's really hard to figure out why people would go to

179

these lengths just for a couple of extra kronor but they do. Every other Swede will save up their empties and just recycle them when they have collected too many for a cupboard to handle, but one thing is for certain, recycling does get done in one way or another.

CLIPBOARDS

If bin scavenging is not for you then you can become one of my most feared marketing employees of all time, the hander-outer/clipboard person.

When I first started living in Gothenburg, there were a number of free newspapers in circulation and the closer you got to the centre, the more likely you were to be handed one. They hunted in packs, and I could never fathom out how to avoid being given at least three newspapers during a simple walk that only took a minute. At one point, I set myself the difficult challenge of making it into Central Station without being handed a free newspaper. I never quite pulled it off, always being caught out by the last defender standing by the traffic lights.

If I tried to alter my route and go through Nordstan shopping centre, I encountered something far worse. Clipboard people. Clipboard people who would ask you if you had time to answer a few simple questions. Clipboard people who also hunted in packs in the same way the newspaper distributors did. Usually, clipboarders worked alone in the UK, making them very easy to avoid. I remember looking at one girl who was holding a clipboard and was drifting in my direction. I took evasive action and drifted in the opposite direction. The girl quickly realised that I was avoiding her and we smiled at each other whilst probably thinking:

Girl: Ah damn! You've spotted me walking towards you. OK. You're avoiding me. Well played.

Me: Oh oh! A clipboarder. If I put enough distance between us, she won't even get to ask her first question. Yep. It worked. Phew!

In Sweden, clipboarders are a hard to avoid. Throw in the newspaper vendors and it could add valuable minutes to your journey. I have broken down the tactics used by these people and they are as follows:

The lone ranger

This lonely vendor works on his own and usually loses out as a result. His or her normal habitats are shopping centres and some busy streets, but they usually fail to get any results. Once side-stepped, you are in the clear, leaving the vendors chasing the wind you leave behind you. Note: The lone ranger usually operates outside of Sweden.

The twins

To try and catch you out, two vendors will stand opposite each other and try to bounce you off one and into the other. The way to combat this is to spot them early and walk through the middle, thus creating a distance equal to both of them. That way, they both have to work hard to get you.

Triple attack

This is where it gets harder. The twin approach is used with the third counteracting your through-the-middle shuffle. To take out the third person, judge the pedestrian traffic by the side of you (usually the left) and start walking at the same pace as a person that is walking up alongside you. This way, the unsuspecting passer-by is used as a bodyguard, being picked off by the third clipboarder.

The hairnet

There's no clear way of getting past the hairnet tactic, as there are usually four or more people in operation here. It's rare but it can happen. There is only one way to deal with this and it's not fool proof. Just walk very fast, waving your hand. This way, it looks as if you are in a hurry to get somewhere. You might get inflicted with the injury of being handed a leaflet if you are unlucky.

GRAFFITI

Another unavoidable aspect of walking through any society is graffiti. Most of it will make areas look dirty and ugly, especially graffiti that is just somebody's tag drawn badly. The first indication that graffiti was different in Sweden came from a trip to a restaurant. Without any clinking of glasses or speeches in earshot, I ate a tasty dinner, washed down with a beer. When nature called, I went to the bathroom only to discover somebody had drawn graffiti all over the mirror. At the time, my Swedish was not perfect but I understood what it said. It contained no swearwords. It wasn't offensive. It wasn't a badly drawn logo although it did convey a message, which was:

"Tack för maten."

Thanks for the food. Thanks for the food? Where did this graffiti artist go to school? It was a far cry from "for free sex ring this number" and "Billy is a wanker". This graffiti vandal seemed to have a conscience. Something to say. They could have said these words to the waiter instead of scrawling it across the bathroom mirror but it was an indication that graffiti was different. Even on the tram, someone had written "love the world" on the seat in front of me. It was about as inoffensive as you could get.

The question "Do you really want to eat fish eggs?" had also been scribbled on an advert for my horror show in a tube, Kalles Kaviar. No badly drawn phallic symbol here as the Swedes obviously have something more serious to say with their graffiti. After all, it is supposed to be an open society where people can voice opinions but I'm not really sure if argumentative graffiti counts. It was certainly different from the "M. Kahn is bent" graffiti of the UK.

NEIGHBOURHOODS

In Gothenburg, I lived in a flat that was considered to be in a slum area. My girlfriend had described the area as being a slum herself, albeit in a jokey way but I was prepared for the fact that it could be rough. I remember thinking about how I could defend myself with the limited judo I had learnt at school, just in case. Maybe I could inflict a Chinese burn on an assailant or maybe a painful pinch of some description but I soon realised, that if I was attacked, it would be hopeless.

A slum in the UK would have meant seeing houses that looked as if they were made out of pebbles, burnt out cars that were still smouldering, a glue-sniffer on every corner and prostitutes not too far away from where they the glue-sniffers were standing. I can imagine a slum being ten times worse than that in the USA.

The slum I moved into in Gothenburg was nothing how I imagined it to be. The ghetto that had been described simply didn't exist. Was this really it? Was this the Bumtown of Gothenburg? Surely not. There were no burnt out cars. I couldn't see any pebbledash houses and I certainly couldn't see any glue vapours disappearing up the nose of any junkie. They could have been lurking around the next corner maybe.

Nope. They simply didn't exist.

An elderly woman moving towards me using a Zimmer frame said "hej" on her way past me. This was hardly the threat of a mugger that wanted to steal my luggage and wear my freshly ironed trousers and boxer shorts. Not even close. Unless pensioners in Sweden had become wise in the art of mugging with a Zimmer frame, or they had adopted some kind of really elaborate pensioner disguise that would have outdone any film make-up artist, they simply didn't exist. Of course, villains existed and it seemed the biggest threat to my safety would be in the centre where a night club had been shot at by some form of mafia. That surely would have worked out worse than being run over by a granny wielding a Zimmer frame or handbag with a brick in it.

THE JACKET MAFIA

Just like the UK, handing in our coats at the entrance at a nightclub and paying a fee for the cloakroom is commonplace. Pubs are devoid of this system and it's your choice if you want to wear your coat all night long. When I lived in Gothenburg, there were many pubs and clubs that had their own jacket taking crew known collectively as the jacket mafia. This even happened in some restaurants as well, which was just beyond any human decency. Imagine, booking an expensive restaurant only to find out that you will charged fifty kronor to hand in your coat. It was your intention to spend a fair amount of money on dinner, but not a charge for somebody to put your coat on a hanger. Sometimes, they didn't even have hangers but pegs instead. It just doesn't make any sense and I objected to going into a restaurant where this service was being forced upon me. I even draw the line at some pubs offering this service. Again, you're going to spend money once you are inside aren't you? There have been some places where I have walked in and kept my coat on, just to spite the jacket mafia who don't deserve fifty kronor for doing a relatively simple task. Now, if they started incorporating a dry cleaning service in with their fifty kronor surcharge then I might be obliged to start rethinking the handing over my coat, but those days won't happen. Only in my dreams.

When challenging the jacket mafia to explain why they charged money to take my coat, they came up with the answer of "fire risk" after scratching their heads for some kind of response. I got the feeling that nobody had ever asked them any questions before and they had to say something to deflect what was clearly a breach of outdoor clothing rights. When asked why I would be considered a fire risk if I entered the bar with my coat on, the jacket mafia got slightly skitty and nervous, laughed and said the same words again – "fire risk". It didn't seem to bother them that putting a substantial amount of coats and garments all in one place would actually help a fire rather than hinder it, and it didn't seem to enter their heads that a non-smoking ban had been enforced. It was their excuse and no explanation was needed.

COATS AND SHOES

This brings me neatly onto my next subject of the

Swedish attitude towards coats and shoes. As we all know, the Swedish weather changes rapidly with the seasons, going from cold in January, to mildly cold towards April, to mildly cold to warm in June, then there's the token two weeks of really hot weather in July before it all goes back to mildly cold, cold and freezing. Now, with these changes in the weather, comes a change with coats and shoes. The Swedes feel that it is necessary to have different coats and shoes for the different times of year. I have never bought so many pairs of shoes and different coats in my life until I had moved to Sweden. Back in the UK, I only bought one pair of shoes and used them until they wore out and let in rainwater, but in Sweden, you'll have so many pairs of shoes that wearing them out will be a thing of the past.

THE LIST OF COATS AND SHOES YOU WILL NEED FOR SWEDEN

1. Coats and shoes for the winter.

It's a fair point. It's cold, icy and the air is full of snow. You'll also need a thick scarf, a pair of gloves and a hat. It's not recommended that you just walk everywhere without them like you would in the UK and almost freeze to death. In fact, you'll probably need winter boots instead of shoes for Sweden. Best make that a pair of shoes and winter boots for this

season. For a coat, you'll need a thick jacket for normal working days and a thick ski-jacket if you do
anything else, especially skiing. Ski-jackets are only
good in times of -20. If it is only -5 for example,
you're best off getting a lighter jacket and wearing
a fleece or cardigan underneath. If you are going to
start going to the gym, as many do in January, you'll
also need some inside gym shoes (this rule also applies in the UK). So you'll need:

1 pair of shoes

1 pair of boots

1 pair of ski boots (if you take up skiing which
you probably will)

1 pair of trainers

1 thick posh jacket

1 ski-jacket

1 lighter jacket with a fleece/cardigan

And for dessert, you'll want gloves, a scarf and a
hat.

2. Coats and shoes for the spring.

As the winter has now passed and it's way too warm
to wear anything you bought in January, you'll have to
buy a standard pair of shoes. You might need anoth-

er pair of trainers to go out in as well. Maybe you'll want to go running or something similar. You'll have to buy a light jacket. Something that is small and not so warm. So you'll need:

1 pair of normal shoes

1 pair of outdoor trainers

A light jacket

3. Coats and shoes for the summer.

Now you're talking. The two weeks of obligatory sunshine has arrived and with it, a bill for more items to clog up your wardrobe. You'll need:

1 pair of sandals

1 pair of light trainers (the ones that let the air in to your feet. They exist believe me.)

1 waterproof jacket (you never know when it will rain in the summer. Best to buy a small jacket that is waterproof with a hood. You know the rubbery type kaguls you used to wear as a kid? That kind of jacket but for.. er hum… adults)

2 caps (always best to have a spare)

4. Coats and shoes for the autumn.

Remember the stuff you bought back in the spring? That doesn't count for autumn as you will

190

need an autumn jacket. Not as light as the one you bought for spring, and not as heavy as the one you bought for winter. Something in-between. You might want to consider getting another pair of shoes for the autumn as well. You'll need them. Here's what you'll need:

1 autumn jacket

1 pair of shoes

So when you add everything up, you should end up with this list for the year:

8 x pairs of shoes

1 x pair of ski boots

6 x coats or jackets

1 x fleece or cardigan (although buying more of these is recommended)

2 caps

1 woolly hat, scarf and gloves

Now multiply everything by two to best represent an approximate figure of what your partner will buy and you'll have a collection of shoes that Imelda Marcos would be jealous of, and a jacket collection that will have the jacket mafia rubbing their hands together whilst rubbing their hands together, expectant of profit.

BINS AND RUBBISH

If you do wear out all your multiple pairs of shoes, or your umpteen coats for that matter, you'll want to know how to dispose of them. Again, in the UK, it was all a case of throwing things in one bin liner and then chucking it out into the street for the rubbish men to collect. Earlier in this book, I briefly mentioned that Sweden was hot on recycling and had different bins for different waste. For any new immigrant to the country, not used to this system, it can be daunting. The first time that I tried to throw away some rubbish was a difficult time for me as my girlfriend would keep stating:

"Not that bin, this bin. Wrong bin. That goes there."

It was difficult to figure out where to throw away my unused tube of banana caviar and various pieces of packaging.

One bin for compost.

One bin for plastics.

One bin for metals.

One bin for coloured glass.

One bin for clear glass.

One bin for used batteries.

One bin for newspapers and magazines.

One bin for cartons and cardboard.

One bin for small electronics.

My God! Sweden had thought of everything here. I'd never had to separate my rubbish in such a neat, orderly fashion before. I hadn't even seen a rubbish man here. Did they even exist? I wasn't sure. Perhaps they operated at night like badgers. I just didn't know. Everything is thrown away in what is called the *miljöhus* or *soprummet* (which translates into the environment house or rubbish room) except larger items that you have to take care of yourself. This task is impossible if you haven't got your own transport as most tips are situated away from public transport stops, and let's face it, if you are throwing something large away, you won't want to heave it onto the trams or tube.

Although you could view this system as really nit-picking at rubbish throwing, it's a huge step towards making progress when it comes to the environment. The UK is slowly moving towards this, but still has a problem with fly-tipping, people dumping things in the wilderness because they don't want to pay council costs to dispose of them in the right way. Although I don't excuse this behaviour, you can understand why some people do it when you take into consideration the story of a friend wanting to throw away a door.

Sounds simple enough, right? Well......

"Hi. Can I arrange an appointment for you to pick up a door I need to throw out?"

"Of course. We can make it on Tuesday and it'll cost 30 pounds".

"30 pounds to take away a door?"

"Yes, sir."

"I thought it would be free. What if I took off the hinges and the handle?"

"Unfortunately not, sir. It's not free. If you take the hinges and handle off, it'll still be a door without its hinges and handle."

"And it would still be 30 quid?"

"Yes, sir."

"What about if I chopped it into 2 pieces?"

"It would still be a door that would be in 2 pieces."

"Still 30 quid?"

"Yes, sir."

"4 pieces and I'll strip the paint off it?"

"That would be fine, sir."

"And free?"

"As long as you have other things for us to collect as well, it will be free, sir."

Do you really think this conversation would happen here in Sweden? I don't think the Swedish would care about the resemblance of something before they considered it worthy to throw away.

NUDITY AND UNDERWEAR

There has probably never been a conversation that I haven't had with Brits about Sweden that didn't contain something about nudity. Every Brit assumes Sweden to be a sex-crazed country full of nymphomaniacs called Sven and Helga. Not so. Home shopping catalogues may feature dildos, skinny dippers might exist, and sex may well be considered natural but this is just Sweden being Sweden. A television commercial featuring a woman pushing a car down the road in her underwear was an eyebrow lifter to English friends who were over for a visit. Conservative attitudes in the UK will be put to the test when they discover that some Swedes won't think twice about walking around in their undies when other people are present. The shock of my life happened when a work colleague opened the door dressed just in his underpants and a toothbrush in his mouth. It was a harmless breakfast call, or so I thought, but it was just an example of Swedes just being Swedes.

It has been also commented upon that Swedes are naturists when it comes to summertime dipping.

It has to be said that I found it almost a shock when I took a tourist boat trip around Stockholm and saw skinny dippers in the middle of the city, not caring about amount of cameras pointed in their direction. Not every Swede will go skinny-dipping. In fact, I think it is only a select few that would choose to do this but nevertheless, it does happen and it might be something you'll see in the summertime.

NOISE POLLUTION & TIME KEEPING

The time is at the core of everything that we do. We wake up at certain times to go to work, meet people at certain arranged times and most of us wear a watch to keep up with it. The only problem with time is that sometimes it can be unacceptable to do certain things. For example, if you live in a flat, there is a 10 p.m. curfew about making noise so as not to disturb the neighbours. This, however, can be overcome by writing a polite note saying that you are, for example, having a party and it will be noisy past 10 p.m.. This note can then be pinned up on a notice board in your building, letting all of your lovely neighbours know this fact and have them still talk to you the following day. The same, however, can't be said about the reverse of this, the unwritten 7 a.m. curfew. Now, don't misread or assume that any of my neighbours have thrown early morning parties at

7 a.m.. They haven't and most likely never will but what I am aiming my gripe at here is construction workers. Both in Gothenburg and Stockholm, construction workers think that it's perfectly ok to start up their machinery, start drilling and banging hammers at 7 a.m.. It has happened to me in both cities and although I usually had to get up for work, I liked to lie in bed until 8 a.m. as I started work at 10 a.m.. After I had been rudely awoken by construction workers at this earlier hour in the day, I was then astonished to find they would stop working at around 9 a.m.. It's as if they do it on purpose to wake everyone up with an attitude of - we got up early and so should you! I think a new rule should be brought in for construction workers where they should have to write a polite note saying - We will be making some noise at around 7 a.m. to wake everyone up and then just to add insult to injury, stop at 9 a.m.. We are sorry for any inconvenience and we're not giving any explanation to why we do this either.

Time keeping is something the Swedes are even hotter about when compared to recycling. If you make an appointment or date with a Swede, turning up late is not acceptable. In fact, Swedes will probably expect you to turn up ten minutes early. It's not easy for an immigrant who has had to learn how to tell the time again and if you have an appointment that is 4.25 p.m. for example, it can be a big problem. I have, on a few occasions, turned up an hour late because I failed to get the time right when arranging it over the phone. It's not easy trying to explain that understanding times is slightly harder than it should be to someone who has been tapping their foot, calling to see where you are and pacing up and down for an hour.

It can work the other way around as well. A simple trip to the cinema almost turned into a disaster when anal time keeping came into play. The doors to the salon were due to be opened at 8:30 p.m. for a film starting at 9:00 p.m.. It sounded fair enough and we had got there slightly early too. My girlfriend was desperate for the toilet and asked the ticket ripping cinema attendant if she could use the toilet that was situated past the gate's cordoned off area. Breathing a sigh, the attendant looked at his watch and then at the clock on the wall that read 8:28 p.m..

"The gate is not open yet so you'll have to wait."

"What? But it's only 2 minutes."

"Sorry," said the king of analness, tapping his watch, "we are closed."

After this conversation had ended, the time reached 8:30 p.m. and he opened the gate anyway but this is a prime example of how hot on time keeping Swedes are.

TOILETS

When you have actually made it to the toilet you'll be glad to know it doesn't cost any extra. Some public toilets, however, will charge 5 kronor and others 10 kronor. That's roughly 50p to £1 per pee or number two. It can come as a bit of shock if you have just moved to a Swedish city, are desperate for a pee, and have no coins. If your bladder is at bursting point, you'll be cursing the fact that you'll be lucky to find a free toilet, and will just have to settle for a tree or bush somewhere, if you can find one. It's fair enough if the actual toilet facility is well looked after, but it can be an expensive business if you want to use a toilet in a city. Taking the piss? Yes, they probably are and they'll charge you to take it from you.

PUBS & CLUBS

A visit to a pub may reward you with a free toilet, but there are other factors that pub visits can throw up. In the UK it is buying rounds. I was never quite sure if it was laziness that started off the trend of doing this rather than separate drinks, but most arguments happen in UK pubs because of these words:

- It's your round!

The person who has just said these three little

words will get some abuse if they have got it wrong and defend themselves if it is actually their round instead. Mistakes inevitably happen when using this system, but usually, if someone buys a round out of turn or by mistake, it's usually just forgotten about and written off by the next time they go out again. This never happens in Sweden because people really hate owing somebody money. If you buy someone a drink, they will just have to buy you one back and if they fail to do that, they'll give you what the drink cost in cash the next time they see you. Even if you have the best intentions of treating someone to a drink and just being nice to them, they'll still feel as if they have to return the favour. It's almost like an insult to them and buying rounds is a definite no no. Swedes usually like to pay their own way in this world.

Keeping on the subject of drinking, a curious event in the middle of the week that happens on Wednesdays, has always left me asking questions as to why it happens - little Saturday. Yes. Wednesdays are called little Saturdays for a reason unknown to me. Although Swedes frown upon having a beer at lunchtime during a working day, it seems perfectly ok to go out drinking in the middle of the week on a Wednesday evening. There's nothing special about a little Saturday. There are no discounted dinners being offered anywhere. There are no afterwork deals happening. There aren't even any two for one deals on drinks. It begs the question - why? I am assuming here that little Saturday must have a counterpart, namely 'hangover Sunday' that actually happens on a Thursday. Then by the time that you are feeling better on Friday afternoon, you have to do it again when 'afterwork Friday' happens, leaving you to recover on 'big Saturday', providing you don't go out again, and 'sober Sunday'.

THE TAX OFFICE

Although owing somebody money is almost a sin in Sweden, when it comes to the tax office, being owed money by them is perfectly ok, especially if you have spent money on redecorating or refurbishing your home or need to claim back travel allowances. When the tax form plops into your letterbox, there is some form of excitement and anticipation in what you will get back or what you'll be able to claim. This excitement and anticipation can turn into dread and fear if you work freelance because you usually end up owing the tax office money instead. For many, the tax form will just be a simple matter of agreeing to whatever the form says and sending a thumbs up back to the tax office. However, for freelancers, this time of year can mean huge headaches as you wade through receipts, extra forms and extra forms for those forms. There'll be so many factors and so many confusing instructions, it'll make you change your tax status, called FA skatt, and get your old working tax status, called A skatt, back again, just to avoid filling in multiple tax forms. Of course, Sweden is not alone in confusing tax forms and tax information. The UK also has them and probably so does every other country. Not even Archimedes would have been able to cope with these fiendishly devised mathematical problems.

PENSIONS

Pensions are another grey area when you are a Swede, let alone an immigrant. Every single year, a large orange envelope will land on your doorstep, telling you what you projected pension will be when you retire. I understood the orange envelope, but didn't understand how the pension was split up into different sections. A pyramid, not made out of shrimps, details your general pension and is based on income and premium pension. For my premium pension, it was up to me to choose where to place my money from a list of bonds and stocks. I had no idea what I was looking at or if it was important to tick a box or not. After much deliberation and cogitation, I decided to just ignore it and hoped it would just go away. After a few weeks, I received a letter through the post stating that I hadn't chosen anything and it would be handled by the state. Although it sounded quite serious, I still really didn't understand anything, so I just ignored this letter as well. After my girlfriend found out what I had done, she quickly reacted and told me that I should have chosen something and it was wrong not to do so. Hanging my head in shame, there was nothing I could do now. The letters had been ignored. My pension was being dealt with. There was no chance of me having any understanding of it. As it turned out, the people who didn't choose anything ended up doing better than those who had. Ignorance is bliss! A financial TV show calmly told the Swedish nation:

"It makes no difference if you choose something or not and usually the best thing you can do is just ignore it."

WHAT YOU HAVE LEARNT FROM THIS CHAPTER

- Bears are not required to carry ID cards but you might find out where they live through the tax office.

- A Swedish hitman's job is a breeze.

- Driving on the left? No winter tyres? Different language? Can you drive in Sweden? Of course! Here's your licence. Varsågod!

- Raffle tickets called nummerlappar are handed out but you won't win anything.

- Speeches happen… clink clink clink… more compared… clink clink clink… to… clink clink clink… I give up!

- Curly sandwiches and sausage rolls are not on the menu.

- Recycling can crush small children.

- Newspaper vendors and clipboarders can make you late for work.

- Graffiti can brighten up your day.

- Mafia extortion happens through threatening coats.

- One pair of shoes and a jacket is not enough.

- Throwing away rubbish requires thought.

- Keeping time can mean waiting up until the last second.

- You can't buy somebody a drink without being owed.

- Tax forms are just as hard to understand in Swedish.

- If you get a large orange envelope through the post that looks important, ignore it.

11. POLITICS

I come from the land of Churchill, Thatcher, and Blair and, therefore, you might assume that I would have a lot to talk about when it comes to politics. There have been so many scandals in the UK involving politicians that you probably won't have enough fingers and toes to count them all. Some scandals turn out to be false allegations but some undoubtedly, and shamefully, turn out to be true. The UK had the Profumo affair in the '60s and Sweden had the Geijer scandal in the '70s so it could be said there are some comparisons to be drawn.

SCANDALS

Scandals very rarely happen within Swedish politics and because of this, when a small story breaks, it has to be blown up into something extraordinary. Mona Sahlin, now ex-leader of the Social Democrats (Labour in the UK), has always been dogged by something called the Toblerone affair, where it was reported that she had bought a bar of Toblerone, nappies and other items on a work-issued credit card. The bill was then settled through receipts and reimbursed to the state. The rules said that the credit card was not to be used for personal use but they also said what to do when it was. What a scandal! If this had happened to Margaret Thatcher, there would have been no scandal at all, and she would have defended herself in no uncertain terms. I can imagine her saying:

- When one feels the need to satisfy one's hunger, one must eat.

She would have used words to that effect and the not so exciting scandal would have been dealt with there and then. It, of course, depends on whether Thatcher liked Toblerone or not. If I were to guess, I would imagine that Thatcher, if she could, would have bought a bag of those red Quality Street chocolates that had the really hard centres. As we all know, Thatcher had something against dairy products and probably would have opted for a nice packet of finger biscuits that she took away from my nursery.

However, no list of scandals would be complete without the mention on the equivalent of the UK's BNP, Sverigedemokraterna (Sweden Democrats), who managed to edge their way into parliament. To best explain how they came to be voted into parliament in the first place, it's probably a good idea to tell you a little bit about how the Swedish parliament system is set up.

POLITICAL SYSTEMS

When one thinks of the UK political system, you really only think of three main parties: Labour, Conservative and Liberal. Although there are other parties such as UKIP and the Monster Raving Loony Party, who at one point had a cat as their leader, there isn't much room for anyone else than the three mentioned, and there isn't much room for one of those either.

When you look at the Swedish system, there are a whole host of local and minor parties out there, all looking to get voters interested in them. If one of these parties gets 4% of the votes, they then get to move into the parliament building and be represented. At the time of writing, nine parties are currently in parliament with - you guessed it - the Social Democrats (Labour) and Moderate Party (Conservative) being the top two. When it comes around to election time, the smaller 4% parties will form a coalition with either the Social Democrats or the Moderate Party, almost making a two choice system. Of course, you can vote for who you want, and if they happen to fall into one these coalitions, the parties will all have to work together to deliver what they promised. As previously mentioned, the Sweden Democrats were voted in in because they amazingly received the magic 4%, later 13%, figure and got into parliament. It was great news for them until they found out that no other party would work with them.

POLITICIANS ON TV

The other main political parties represent green politics, social liberalism, centerism, socialism and Christian democracy. The leaders of each party will, more than likely, turn up on TV at some point in time, arguing with another politician, in a controlled manner, on debate shows that are popular in Sweden. It's not unlike the UK, but when politicians start turning up on other shows you start to see differences. Some of the party leaders have appeared on talk shows in the same vein as *Parkinson*, whereas others have turned up on satirical comedy shows, in sketches. It's hard to imagine any of the leaders of the current political parties in the UK doing this although, in the past, Neil Kinnock did turn up in a Tracy Ullman video, and the late Charles Kennedy was a guest on some satirical shows. Acting and starring in sketches? It's not something we are completely used to in the UK with our stiff upper lips and moderate conservatism. Swedes got to experience the stiff upper lip when journalist, Stina Dabrowski interviewed Margaret Thatcher. At the end of the show, Stina had invented her own jump trademark, where she would ask whoever she had interviewed to do a small jump to be freeze-framed. Margaret Thatcher's upper lip turned out to be stiffer than concrete, and she refused to jump, becoming the only person in the history of the show not to do so.

"I make great leaps forward, not little jumps in studios," replied Margaret Thatcher.

No matter how much Stina tried to convince the Iron Lady to do the jump, including stating that Gorbachev had done it, she refused point blank describing the whole thing as "puerile" and just something that people do to become popular. Whether or not Thatcher was right to refuse is debatable, but this act of defiance became synonymous with Thatcher.

Swedish politicians, in my opinion, are more approachable probably because of the open society Sweden has but also because some of them look as if you could just hang out with them. They'll appear on TV wearing jeans and a jacket, making them look fairly relaxed and, dare I say it, normal. Britain's politicians have, mostly, prided themselves on having a dry-cleaned suit pressed for the working day ahead. It's not often that you'll see them wearing jeans and acting chilled out.

THINGS YOU HAVE LEARNT FROM THIS
CHAPTER
209

- A bear would make a good leader for the Monster Raving Loony Party.

- Swedish political scandals can involve chocolate.

- Swedish politicians work together like one big happy family.

- Politicians can be chilled out and get away with it.

- Margaret Thatcher didn't jump for anybody.

12. SPORT & FITNESS

You remember how I spoke about everybody being equal and nobody loses? Sport is the only exception to this rule because in the big wide world outside of Sweden, people lose. If you lose a race on school sports day in the UK, you suck. If you finish second in a race on school sports day, you still suck but not as much as finishing last.

ROUNDERS AND BURNBALL

Before I approach the subject of serious sports and athletes, I want to talk about the less harmful fun sports that we used to play in school in the UK. Rounders was always the game to play and I always saw it as a less serious version of baseball. The mission was to hit a freshly bowled ball into the sky and at a distance, run around four bases that were laid out in a sort of wonky circle and score a run. If a fielder caught the ball, you were out. If a fielder threw the ball to a base-keeper before you reached it, you were out. If you were out, it probably meant you sucked at this game. If you scored a run and joined the back of the queue of batters, you were probably really good at all sports, just based on this fact.

Now, imagine if you will, the game of rounders minus a bowler, minus that caught out rule and minus the base-keeping rule. If you can imagine all that, you have the Swedish counterpart of *brännboll*, which translated means burnball. You might be under the impression that *brännboll* is a really violent version of rounders, after all, it is call *brännboll*. Is it a ball that is bowled so fast, it can actually burn you if it hits you and not your bat? Do they set balls on fire and then use them? No. *brännboll* is a game where you bowl the ball to yourself by throwing it up into the air and the hitting it. Now your opposing team may get another fielder out of this, but it has always felt odd to bowl the ball to myself when playing. Call me a traditionalist but a bowler just feels natural to a game like this one. Could you imagine baseball having the same rule? There would be home runs aplenty but would be painfully boring to watch.

Once you have pelted the ball as hard as you can, you won't be out of the game if the fielders catch it without it hitting the ground. You won't be out if the fielder returns the ball to a brännare (burner) and to a base (called kon in Swedish) before you reach it. When I first played the game, I actually wondered if anyone actually loses because as far as I could see, if nobody could be caught out of the game and keep batting, the Swedes really would be sticking to their nobody loses rule. So what is the game of *brännboll* all about when nobody can be caught or go out? It all boils down to points. If a brännare gets the ball before you reach the base and stamps on the burn pad (brännplatta), the batting team loses points and has to go back the previous base and run when the next person hits the self-bowled ball. The fielding team wins points through catching the ball with one hand or two hands. So although it's impossible for a player to be out of the game, you'll be booed if you lose points or burnt as the game is so aptly named. It's not quite the fact that nobody loses in this game; it's just made to feel that way especially to outsiders to Sweden.

KUBB

Another harmless game is called *Kubb*, which is played in the summer, usually on a beach and after consuming some beers and badly charcoaled barbecued food. I won't go into the rules too much, but I will say that it involves throwing sticks, which you have to make spin vertically at your opponents blocks on the other side in a bid to knock them over. The team will then throw them back, trying to knock the other team's blocks over. There's a little bit more to this game than I am letting on, but once a team hasn't got any opponent blocks to knock down, they can aim for the king block in the middle of the playing area. Once the king has fallen, that team wins, along with retiring for more beer and more food that resembles carbon. The only rule that exists with this game is that the more you drink, usually the more entertaining it gets because by the end of the barbecue, nobody can throw straight any more. In English terms, think of this like a cross between skittles and bowling.

Bowling is spelt the same way in Swedish as it is in English, but because W is an unofficial letter, the Swedes pronounce it *bovling* instead, making it sound like a game that uses gravy granules in some way. It's unclear why the Swedes chose to keep the W and spell it the same way as the English do when W really doesn't exist, but they have and it's *bovling* to them.

The game of boule, or pétanque, is very popular in Sweden with new boule bars opening up steadily. However, some of the boule bars do not have the flat playing surface that many boule players are accustomed to, making the game more of a challenge. Just when you think your boule is on course to kiss the jack, a bump in the ground will bounce it into no man's land, leaving you cursing about your failed throw. I think this is an attempt to straighten out a person's throw when they have drunk too much.

SWEDEN BEATS NORWAY

Small, fun games are fine and well, but when it comes to the more potential medal winning sports, the nobody loses attitude can change to the so-long-as-we-beat-Norway attitude. Nowhere is this more apparent than winter sports where Norway are seen as the big wigs, but now and again, a Swede will creep onto the top spot of the podium to ruin their day. If this happens, Swedish TV will show this feat happening over and over again in re-runs, in repeat shows, at award ceremonies and just showing it again whenever they can. There must be some theory that this might not be achieved again for a while so we'd better milk it for what it's worth, but it gets irritating when you hear the same commentary time and time again. For example:

- Härligt! Härligt! Vi har vunnit guld! HALLÅ! VI HAR VUNNIT GULD!

This is a standard phrase when a Swede wins anything, but it's mostly said during world championships or the Olympics. Of course, the UK has its own phrasing too so there's no real difference between them other than the fact that clips of gold winning Swedes seem to be repeated far more often.

If, God forbid, a Swede fails to win a medal and really screws up his or her chances because of a mistake, the tabloids will always use the same word they use for the Eurovision – fiasco.

215

WINTER SPORTS

When it comes to winter sports, I will always stick up for the Swedes because Sweden has become my home and, let's face it, the UK isn't famed for its winter athletes with Conrad Bartelski being the last man to finish on the podium in 1981, and that was nothing short of a miracle. It's hardly surprising, when you think about it, when five millimetres of snow is enough to bring the UK to a complete standstill. We just don't know what to do with it. If the UK is to be remembered for winter sports, poor Conrad is usually overlooked because of Eddie "the eagle" Edwards, probably one of the worst ski-jumpers to ever live. That's what the UK is famed for in the winter Olympics. A short-sighted ski jumper who named himself after a graceful bird of prey, something he fell well short of both in terms of achievements, and in actual distance. On the other hand, I couldn't imagine doing a ski jump myself and the fact that he jumped off cardboard boxes in his back garden meant that he probably couldn't imagine it either. He had a go. He failed. He will be remembered for it.

There is a winter sport that is even crazier than skiing down a mountain and off the side of a cliff – the winter triathlon. Many countries take part in what must be one of the most gruelling winter sports out there where competitors run, cycle, and then go cross-country skiing. I can't imagine going out for a run in snow and ice even if I had spiky shoes. A trip to the supermarket had me flat on my face in the car park, and then if that wasn't bad enough, a speeding car splattered me with slush. That would put me off doing any type of running in the winter, not as if I was going to anyway. It's like comparing cycling through snow to running on a Velcro track wearing thick woolly socks. If the first two tasks hadn't turned the competitor's legs into lactic acid, then the third task of skiing will comfortably finish them off by the time they cross the finish line. I prefer watching the triathlon in my warm, cosy home with a mug of tea rather than having a go myself. It's exhausting enough watching them let alone doing it. The same goes for the summer triathlon that replaces skiing with swimming, which looks to be just as gruelling.

Summer or winter triathlons are not the hardest events in the Swedish sporting calendar. Sweden plays host to the longest cross-country skiing race in the world called *Vasaloppet*. At 90km long (56 miles), people come from all over the world to take part in the race, inspired by a run King Vasa did in 1520. Compared to the UK, the London marathon is considered a long race at less than half the distance and even if Brits were allowed to use their car, a 56-mile drive would still have most believing that it would be a 'bit of a drive'. Whether or not Swedes win at the Olympics, the winter Olympics, world championships or *Vasaloppet*, they take sport as seriously as other countries do.

HORSES

The Grand National is the most famous horse race in the UK mainly because of its four miles of unforgiving fences of which there are thirty, sixteen fences jumped twice expect two. Although animal activists have been trying to stop the race claiming brutality, the Grand National has been the one horsing event that many will take a flutter on. The horse, Red Rum, who won the race three times and finished second twice, became the symbol of horse racing. Merchandise with his image were made, books were written about him, and he even opened supermarkets by way of guest appearances. Red Rum must have had trouble using the scissors to cut the ribbon, but nevertheless, this horse was as much a celebrity as *Mr. Ed* was.

The names of horses can be just as funny in Sweden as the UK, but one of the most popular form of horse racing is harness racing. The jockeys sit in a two-wheeled cart behind the horse with their legs spread wide in a V shape. This may eliminate getting saddle sore, but I'm sure another description of what pain they must go through exists. If sitting with your legs spread as wide as they can go is bad enough, the jockeys also have to endure being pebble dashed and splattered with mud from the circuit and anything the horses might do whilst running. The jockeys are sometimes interviewed after a race and the only part of them you can usually see are their eyes when they lift their visor up.

SPEEDWAY

Another sport that involves going round in circles on two wheels is speedway. This involves four trial bikes that whizz around on a muddy circuit, jostling for the lead. They do this probably for the same reason that the jockeys do – to avoid being sprayed with mud. If they had really thought about it, they could have killed two birds with one stone and attach the carts from the horse racing to the bikes. After all, the riders and jockeys are getting splattered with the same mud, minus what the horses do. They still get to go round in circles but replace the horses with horsepower.

ORIENTEERING

Contact with mud is not just confined to horses and motorbikes. Some people go out into the wilderness, running through forests, looking for control points in the form of orienteering. Although popular with quite a large number of Swedes, most people had large question marks over their heads when an orienteering gold medal winner was nominated for a sports award.

- Oh! Did Sweden win a gold in orienteering then?

As popular as it is, it's very rarely televised and if it is, it's not on a time when people can watch due to work. So when an orienteerer's name popped up at this particular awards ceremony, a comment of - well done but we had no idea - was whispered by most.

FITNESS

For anyone wanting to get into sports, Sweden is a good place to start because of the mass of open space that is easy to jog or run through. Taking up skiing is also possible, but you have to be prepared to fall over a fair number of times if you have never tried it before. I spent a good hour with my face in the snow before I understood that it was all about balance. I certainly had more respect for downhillers when I couldn't even ski on flat land, couldn't turn corners or, in fact, stop either. When the heavens open and the snow colours the land white, people generally grab their skis, travel to the nearest field and go hell for leather. The very first track that I visited, bearing in mind that I hadn't skied before, was in a place a fair distance from Stockholm City.

It had been recommended so we packed our skis and headed to it. I was quickly introduced to almost professional skiers going round in tight fitting latex outfits, looking at stopwatches. It wasn't for the faint hearted, and it certainly wasn't for beginners as I found out when I kept falling over. Speeding skiers swerved to the left and right, avoiding my sorry carcass that was buried deep in the snow. I knew that this wasn't the place for any beginner to try out. It was here that I coined the phrase - an Englishman on skis is a health hazard. The stopwatches were a dead giveaway that something serious was happening on this track but it's not been the only time I have seen them.

Eriksdalsbadet in Stockholm is the largest swimming complex in Sweden, offering the services of an Olympic sized swimming pool to the public. There is one drawback to this. It's not that it is exceptionally busy. It's because wannabe Sarah Sjöströms bring their personal trainers plus those stopwatches to the pool. Whenever I have wanted to use the larger pool, I have had to stop because of all the trainers darting about, following their new potential Olympic medal winning swimmer up and down the lanes. There have been times when I just wanted to enter the pool to see what would happen, but thought better of it and opted for the jacuzzi instead.

PUBLIC GYM SAUNAS

You may find people with personal trainers at Swedish gyms, but this is largely expected at most gyms worldwide. People that go to the gyms are also largely the same. The guy that stays on one machine, going red in the face, moaning, gritting his teeth and straining because he is lifting way too much, also exists in Swedish gyms. There's no escaping him.

Saunas are the real difference between UK and Swedish gyms. I was told that taking a sauna after a workout was the thing to do when I first starting going to the gym again. Taking that advice onboard, I walked into a sauna for the first time after a particularly easy-going workout. There were already two or three naked men in there with towels but that was ok I thought as I ventured in. Quickly realising how stuffy it was and how hot it was, it wasn't long before I was gasping for some fresh air and left the sauna after about ten seconds, much to the amusement of the expert sauna users. After a while, I did become used to the sauna, and now use one all the time when I finish a workout, but you do meet some curious people in them at times. There was one time where I was minding my own business, zoning out and relaxing when a guy opened the door and asked if he could add water to the coals. I didn't see any harm in this so I just nodded and agreed with him, thinking he would use the normal bucket and ladle. However, when he opened the door again, he was armed with a sponge on a stick and a bucket of water. I suddenly became slightly worried as he started to climb on the benches and began painting the walls. Looking at him in a slightly confused way, he explained that it was all to do with moisture; moisture was the key to a successful sauna session. Moisture. Moisture. After he had made sure to cover the walls with make believe paint, he left the sauna again, leaving me to relax momentarily for a few minutes until he came back armed with a hosepipe. His explanation for this new addition to the sauna certainly had nothing to do with moisture. This had to do with a huge amount of heat that rose from the coals as he unloaded a jet of water onto them. I remembered that I had agreed for him to throw some more water on the coals but not complete saturation. As the heat started to rise quicker than my cooker plates at home on full power, I felt the oxygen levels were not sufficient for my need to breath, and I opted to leave very quickly. As the painter man sat down with his sponge on a stick and bucket, I said goodbye in a sarcastic way, leaving him to fry in his own furnace. He certainly must have been in training for some sort of sauna competition because I have never encountered anyone else wanting a sauna as hot as a kiln before. I have also not seen any people hit each other with twigs either which seems a more common past time in Finland than Sweden.

Remember how I said jockeys were punished by being pelted with mud? Well, for Swedes that are not jockeys, there is a form of punishment that they can give themselves if the mood takes them. The next step up from a sauna, if you really want to give yourself the whole experience, is to go and jump into an icy pool of water. Deep in the heart of winter, when lakes are frozen over, and the sea has trouble moving, a party of people somewhere, is indulging in this activity. Replacing their nice, cosy warm sauna for a dash outside in minus temperatures, a hop into icy water and then back into the sauna again. For people that haven't tried this, it appears to be complete lunacy on the part of crazy Swedes, but for those who have tried this, they will tell you that it is an experience worth taking part in. On one level, I can understand that exposing the body to extreme warmth and then extreme cold can be good for blood circulation, but on another level, taking a dip in ice is a bit too extreme for me. I remember being given those puffy Eskimo suits for the ice bar in Gothenburg at Liseberg…

FOOTBALL

The football season in the UK is played during the winter months, exposing footballers to icy conditions. The Swedish football season is played throughout the summer months through to the start of winter, smartly avoiding the bad weather and potential postponed games.

There have been a multitude of Swedish football players that have made their way into UK teams and although Swedish football is extremely popular, Swedes will also have their favourite British side. It has been my experience, when watching my team in action in the F.A. Cup, that Swedes will tend to favour a Premiership side as their team of choice over their Swedish counterpart. It's a strange feeling when a Swede will admit that their team is also West Ham. I always question them why that is, when West Ham is the furthest away from what I would imagine a Swede would like in terms of football teams. The usual response to this is "why not?" Maybe it has something to do with the team's colours, or the fact that Freddy Ljungberg did a stint for them, or that they just like the way they play. It always baffles me.

Other sports like ice hockey and handball are very popular alongside a curious game called bandy. If you imagine ice hockey stretched out of proportion with larger goals, larger pitch and more players with the rules of football, it's a fairly accurate description of what bandy is. Bandy can be played outdoors and indoors in the same way that football can be and is sometimes shown on TV. When indoor football was shown on Northampton's local TV channel, they forgot to turn off the cameras at half time and caught the players have a quick smoke before continuing on with the second half. Sport loving Swedes who play indoor bandy would probably not be caught doing this.

WHAT YOU HAVE LEARNT FROM THIS CHAPTER

- Jumping in an icy lake is for polar bears.

- *Brännboll* favours self-bowling.

- *Kubb* favours the sober.

- Indoor boule favours the drunk.. sometimes.

- As long as Sweden beats Norway, it's a win.

- Just watching triathlons is exhausting.

- Horses can open supermarkets.

- Jockeys and speedway riders love mud.

- Stopwatches mean trouble for beginners.

- Saunas are hot. Freezing lakes are cold. Let's do both.

- West Ham is the team to support in Sweden.

- Smoking whilst playing sport is the opposite of a performance enhancing drug.

13. TRAVEL, HOLIDAYS

& TOURISTS

Travelling in the UK is a challenge regardless if you have chosen public transport or travel by car. I come from a town near Milton Keynes, and there is no other prime example of how driving can be challenging to a tourist on holiday.

ROUNDABOUTS

Milton Keynes is laid out on a grid system and is divided up by roundabouts that all have a letter and a number, for example J8. There are road signs to help you get to where you are going, but when most roundabouts look the same, and happen every five minutes, a tourist to the area might get confused. B1, F3, J8, B1, A2.. oh.. we've been here haven't we?

In some form of cruel motoring punishment, the UK also has devised other such roundabout devices to make our life simpler, or at least that was the intention with the magic roundabouts of Hatfield and

Swindon. When you first drive towards the magic roundabouts in these areas, and see the road sign for it, it will look like spiders mating. There's a main roundabout with eight or more smaller roundabouts around the outside of it that'll remind you of the old Mexicans peeing in a bucket joke. Panic and confusion will set in once you are in the queue to negotiate this torture device, with cars coming left, right and centre at you. It boggles the mind to how this roundabout solves anything and how the word magic could be related to it.

Sweden is more relaxed in its approach to driving by using slow, curving roads rather than using roundabouts aplenty. Don't get me wrong, roundabouts exist in Sweden, but when it comes to turning off a main road or motorway, they have turned their back on them and made it fairly simple to drive to your destination.

AUTOMATIC HEADLIGHTS

My first trip to Sweden in 2002 was an eye-opener in terms of driving. It was in the middle of summer, a bright, burning sun was out, illuminating the open road for all to see. As the sightseeing drive commenced, I remarked that a stupid motorist had left his headlights on. After that, I noticed that the car behind had also left its headlights on. I had not noticed that Swedish people were that forgetful but I couldn't quite figure out why everybody had their headlights on in the blazing sun, including the car I was travelling in. The explanation, I was told, was due to the large amount of country roads that dart and cut through forests, making them dark and treacherous to navigate without them. Swedes have thought of everything haven't they? Winter tyres, automatic headlights, and how to run over an elk. They have really spent some time thinking about a motorist's journey.

TRAFFIC

The lack of traffic on the motorways also gave me something to think about. A journey from my hometown to London was fraught with the danger of traffic jams and possible accidents. The town of Luton is notorious for traffic jams and roadworks, and if you are not held up here, then you have done well. Usually, Luton will mean tapping your fingers on the steering wheel and listening to a bad radio station.

There didn't seem to be any traffic in Sweden, and therefore any hold-ups on the road we were travelling on. In fact, the motorway became so quiet at one point that we were the only car on it. This would never happen in the UK. You count yourself lucky if you have a car's length in front of you when travelling in the UK.

ROAD SIGNS

Variable speed limits happen in both countries with the Swedes making some areas slower than others whilst the UK just randomly digs up the tarmac somewhere and lays out cones. You might see signs on UK motorways that read:

- This sign is not use.

When I read this, I thought it was blatantly obvious that the sign was in use because I had just read it. There are probably many more examples of odd UK road signs, but there don't seem to be any in Sweden that don't make any sense. The only road sign that I thought sounded funny was *piggdekk* when driving to and through Norway. I couldn't figure out what it meant. Did it have something to do with pigs not allowed on decking whilst driving? Were they not allowed in Norway at all? It was quickly explained to me that this meant that motorists had to pay a fee for using winter tyres with studs in the city of Oslo. That cleared that up.

You may have noticed that I mentioned a drive to Norway. People in Sweden think nothing of the drive from Stockholm to Gothenburg or Gothenburg to Oslo. Both are roughly four to five hours long and 500km (310 miles) long. Can you imagine the same journey happening in the UK? Conversations with my parents about the trips I made to and from Stockholm to Gothenburg just have them shaking their head in a you're-crazy way. You see, a two-hour drive is a bit of a distance in the UK, whereas it would be a trip to the shops for some in Sweden. A five-hour drive would be considered mental institution territory, and a ten-hour drive would be off the scale of any comprehension.

THE SWEDISH MILE

No chapter in this book would be complete without mentioning a way in which Swedes have come up with a system to best confuse any new British immigrant that has just moved to the country. In previous chapters, I mentioned learning how to tell the time again, and learning the note H in music. You might be dreading what I am about to tell you. The Swedish mile. Sit back and relax while I tell you about this little kiddy.

A Swedish mile is the equivalent to ten kilometres, which converts to 6.2 miles in English terms. Now, this comes with its own problems when somebody will say:

- We're going to drive to Gothenburg today. It's fifty miles away.

231

Any British immigrant to Sweden will think to themselves that they were sure Gothenburg was a lot further away from Stockholm than fifty miles. Commercials advertising a theme park or ski resort will sometimes write the distance in Swedish miles rather than kilometres, probably in an effort to say that it's not far away at all. Thirty miles. It's not far at all. Yes it is. Don't try and trick us. Sometimes, you can't help but fall for it.

Longer journeys would not be complete without the trusty service station and both countries have their fair share of them dotted around the motorways. However, there are differences here as well.

UK SERVICE STATION EXPERIENCES

When I came back from my holiday in 2002, after experiencing cleaner air and some fantastic food, I collected my car from Stansted airport and began my ninety-minute journey home. A fair distance into the journey, I felt my throat closing up from the carbon monoxide from the traffic, which was mostly made up of lorries. A service station was coming up and it seemed like a good idea to stop, if only to buy some water. By the time I had entered the building, food seemed like a good idea, so I grabbed my plastic tray and stood in line. Nothing on the menus looked appetising, but I went through with my order and took the old English classic, fish and chips. The sleepy eyed assistant scooped up some chips and tonged up a battered fish onto my plate, avoiding the slice of lemon that had been resting on it. She served me the plate without looking at me or saying anything. It had probably been a long day for her by the looks of things, but something forced me to entice some speech out of her. She had forgotten the lemon.

"Excuse me. Could I have some lemon please?"

"Wha'?"

"Some lemon. Could I have some lemon please?"

I pointed to the lemon slice that she had ignored earlier.

"Oh. Erm. Well. You can't have that. It's the only slice of lemon we have."

I couldn't help but laugh. A service station that sold fish and chips by the proverbial bucketful that didn't have any lemons? Correction. They had one lemon slice. It must have been an endangered fruit in this part of England, I thought, as I kept looking at the assistant. It was obvious that this last lemon slice had been an ornament up until this point in time. It was a battle of wills, which I'm glad to say I won. She reluctantly picked up the last available lemon slice and added it to my plate.

As I sat down with my greasy meal that could have been doing the backstroke in the large amount of fat on the plate, I noticed a waitress attending to a table next to me. She was middle aged with a cigarette hanging loosely out of her mouth (this was before the non-smoking rule came into effect) and spoke with a cockney accent.

"Awight love. What can I get ya?" she said. A dash of ash hit the floor.

It so far removed from the service stations that I had been to in Sweden. This was almost like a welcome home for me, a shock to the system.

SWEDISH SERVICE STATION EXPERIENCES

I am going to start with probably the worst example of comparison when it comes to Swedish service stations. One of the first that I stopped off in Sweden is called Gyllene Uttern (Golden Otter) in Gränna, featuring a beautiful looking rustic four-star hotel, overlooking a lake. I did say this was the worst possible comparison. For lunch, I ate a perfectly formed professional sandwich, served with a mineral water by staff that waited the table, asking if I was satisfied with everything. Chomping on my perfect sandwich, that came with a non-ornamental lemon on the side, I looked at the view of the lake and thought it was really something. If all service stations were as luxurious as this one, I was going to start travelling more.

Unfortunately, I have not been to another Swedish service station that compares to Gyllene Uttern, but I have to say that half of them serve up decent food, in funky looking buildings with decent drinks. Decent. Of course, some service stations are better than others, and it's just luck of the draw where you decide to stop. Some have funny names like Rattugglan, which is probably a pun on "nattugglan" which means night owl with ratt translating to steering wheel. It certainly makes a change from the name of the area and writing 'services' after it, as so often happens in the UK.

PUBLIC TRANSPORT

Travelling within cities is where Sweden has it made. I mentioned Swedish efficiency when it comes to time keeping and it's very apparent when dealing with public transport. Usually, everything runs on time unless bad weather has made it nearly impossible. It has happened, on occasion, that I have waited for a bus in my hometown for forty minutes only for it to not turn up at all. There's nobody to tell you that this is going to happen and you won't get any compensation for it either. This doesn't happen in Sweden. Loud speaker systems, that look like something out of a boot camp, have been installed to announce cancelled or late trams, tubes and buses and even if you are late, you can claim money back if you are a certain amount of minutes over. As I have said before, Swedes have thought of everything.

Gothenburg was the first city where I had to negotiate public transport, which was made up of buses and trams. Looking at the complexity of tram tracks, driving in Gothenburg can be difficult. Trams weave and warp their way through the city, and can make a new motorist to the centre disorientated. The last thing you want to happen is to be hit by a tram because there won't be much left of your car if it does.

One single fare in Gothenburg covers you for ninety minutes, which is more than ample time to get from one place to the next. Back in Northampton, once you have got off a bus, that's the end of your journey. There are no such luxuries as transfers and you certainly don't get ninety minutes of travel. Just to rub the UK's nose in it a bit more, you can also transfer your journey to a ferry and go to the islands off the coast of Gothenburg, all on one fare. You read that right. One fare. You just can't imagine this happening in London could you?

Just before you finish the cries of - Blimey! That's good, innit? - the fare does come with some responsibility as I found out on a journey on a tram. Halfway through, the tram was suddenly invaded by badge wielding warriors, waging war on non-paying travellers who had to pay a hefty fine for not producing a valid ticket. One guy in the seat in front of me got caught out and used the old trick of pretending to be a foreigner.

"No sir. I speak not Sweeedish."

After a lengthy explanation, the guy was let off. It worked! That sort of tactic would never have worked in the UK. The badge-wielding warriors of the tube take their job really seriously. Too seriously. I remember losing my underground card once and tried to go through the gate, where some inspector saw me:

"Hold on! Hold on! Stop right there! We've got a jumper! We've got a jumper!" said the inspector, talking into his shirt collar.

I'm surprised alarms didn't go off or a metal cage came down from the ceiling, trapping me to the station platform. I was later frowned upon in a menacing way, interrogated to where I had been, and made to pay for my tube ticket again. That day, a criminal was born.

No such day for me in Gothenburg. I gladly showed my 100-card ticket (100 kronor cards were sold in Gothenburg before recently moving to chargeable cards) as having been stamped and rested in my seat.

"Vad har du gjort här?" asked the ticket warrior.

"Sorry? I don't speak Sweeedish" I said, nervously and quite shocked.

"You have pressed 1 instead of 2," said the ticket warrior, looking down at me.

What did this mean? I had got it right. I was just one person and not two as far as I knew.

"I pressed 1 for 1 person. Isn't that right?" I asked.

"No. It's not. That is only one coupon."

The coupon system that is no longer used in Gothenburg featured a green box with buttons one to ten on them. When you rammed your card in the top of the machine, it assumed that you knew what all of these buttons actually stood for and were supposed to press two for a normal trip in the city zone. It was unbeknown to me that I had bought a coupon? I thought they were things you cut out of magazines or got sent through direct mail. What was the ticket inspector on about?

"Coupons?" I quizzed.

"Yes. You see. Coupons. 1 coupon for old people. 2 for normal".

Before further ado, he stamped my ticket with another coupon and went on his merry way.

"Shit!" I thought as he disappeared to tackle more unhappy tram people, "Lucky he didn't check all my previous tickets!"

After I had disembarked from the tram and the ticket inspectors, I walked around the centre of Gothenburg for a while, looking for music shops that sold music in the key of H.

I walked around for forty-five minutes and didn't find a music shop, so I hopped back on the tram, well within my ninety-minute limit. One stop later, it happened again. Ticket warriors. Not again. This was silly. It didn't make any difference this time. I had paid and my ticket was valid. As I handed my ticket over, I knew I was safe.

"Du måste stämpla byte," said the ticket nazi.

"I don't speak Sweeedish," I replied.

"Oh. You must stamp byte. Errrr, byte means.. Swapping."

Without further ado, he whipped my ticket into the machine and pressed the white byte button, which seemed to have no effect on my 100-card whatsoever.

What the hell was this system? I got ninety minutes but it seemed I had to do a lot for it. I had to consult it at all times and keep it up to date. Almost a diary of my travels. This was a lot to ask of a fare. I shrugged my shoulders as the ticket nazi went past and I got off the tram a few stops later. It was hardly worth the aggravation.

In Stockholm, they have all the forms of transport you can shake a stick at including buses, the tube, trams and ferries, although you have to pay extra to use some of the ferries as they are not included in your normal fare unlike Gothenburg. When you wait for a bus in Stockholm, you might detect an odd, sweet, but nasty smell in the air. It's not the cinnamon buns from any bakery but the strange exhaust from ethanol buses as they whizz by. You might find that the drivers themselves are cranky, and asking them any kind of question that might delay them will aggravate them even more. For example, you might want to ask:

- Does this bus go to Nacka?

To which you might get the reply:

- Ingen aning.

This means no idea. At this point, being a customer wanting to go somewhere, I would be worried if a bus driver had no idea where they are driving a bus. Perhaps the drivers have really long days, or have been sniffing up ethanol fumes for too long, but don't be surprised if they aren't as helpful as they should be in Stockholm.

THE TUBE AND TRAINS

The tube and tram drivers, however, don't have the problem of dealing with the public much but they do try to neutralise situations by using the tannoy system. The trains themselves are larger and spacious compared to London's underground, and getting around is easier because Stockholm only has three tube lines. The blue and red lines are mostly underground with most of the stations looking like caves rather than tube stops. To make the stops more aesthetically pleasing, Stockholm chooses to display artworks where they can, on the walls and by escalators. You'll never see a statue of a penguin with a box on its stomach in one of the tube stops in London, not unless it is someone dressed up as one, playing a saxophone in the entrances or exits.

With artworks and penguins aside, there is one major difference between the Stockholm tube and the London underground. It has nothing to do with not making eye contact with fellow passengers that still applies in Stockholm, although you are more likely to strike up a conversation here than you are in London. What I am talking about is the tube voice-over. In Stockholm, you'll hear:

"Tänk på avståndet mellan vagn och plattform när du stiger av."

It's a fairly long-winded way of saying London's effort:

"Mind the gap."

That's it. Just three words do the job in London whereas you would think the voice-over is trying to have a conversation with you in Stockholm.

Sweden's commuter and long distance trains also

241

have their little quirks. The long distance trains can do the Stockholm-Gothenburg run in three hours flat and these are known as the fast trains. Even if you buy a 2nd class ticket on one of these, you'll be treated to a reclining seat and power source for a laptop if you wish to watch a movie or work. That is unless you are one of the people that become sick on these trains. If you are, then using a laptop and eating anything from the bistro may well be out of bounds for you, as you'll be trying to shut your eyes and will be too busy trying to avoid using the sick bags. You see, these trains travel at such a speed on old tracks that they lean around the corners, making some people feel sick. Luckily, I'm not one of those people and can thankfully keep all my wits about me while I travel. The only time when I can feel the train's speed is when I have to buy food from the bistro and then make my way back to my seat. It's not easy carrying a small pile of sandwiches and two cups of hot liquid, even if you do have a cardboard holding box. It's not so easy even without the food and you will find yourself using passenger seats for supports, swinging like a gorilla from headrest to headrest, trying to keep yourself on your feet.

There's nothing too dissimilar about the commuter trains between the UK and Sweden apart from the UK's knack of confusing passengers. One example of this comes from my hometown when I wanted to travel to London. The train had pulled up to the platform and waited for people to board. When the train was filled up with people, an announcer calmly spoke over the tannoy:

"We have an important announcement to make. The front part of the train will be departing at 09:05 for Birmingham. The back part of the train will be departing at 09:10 for London."

Passengers looked at each other confused. Panic ensued. The empty platform became quite crowded as people looked at the train, trying to figure out which part was the front and which was the back. It was hard to tell. It might as well have been a two-headed zebra that you see in trick photographs. This situation then turned into a betting game, as people selected what they thought was their train and hoped for the best. This has not happened to me in Sweden as they tend not to split trains in half.

Swedish commuter trains go where they say they are going to go, although they can stop halfway because of a fault on the track sometimes. If you want to avoid throwing up on the fast trains, you can take the normal commuter train jokingly known as *snigeltåg*, which translated means 'snail train'. It takes five hours for the Stockholm-Gothenburg *snigeltåg* to complete its journey and you may not be guaranteed a seat on it either. When you book a ticket, you might have an option to book a seat, but if you don't, you will be able to sit where you want until someone comes along and says - that's my seat. You'll then have to move all your belongings and find another

243

seat only for the same thing to happen again. When I have booked a seat on these trains, I have always ended up in what is called the communal room, a small section of the train where the seats are built facing each other in an enclosed space. Now, I don't know if it is me or not but whenever I have ended up in this part of the train, there is always someone with a large dog opposite me and a guy snoring his head off in the next seat. So if you want to try and make the five hours pass quicker by sleeping, you can forget it if you have the throat and nose choir in concert practicing in the cabin.

SWEDES AND BRITS ON HOLIDAY

"Señor Svensson. Señor Svensson. Please come to reception," bellowed the receptionist at Gran Canaria's airport.

Little did she know what she had done when her front desk was under siege by a large number of sun-tanned, slightly hung-over, tall blue-eyed Swedish men wanting to know why she had called their name out.

When on holiday, Swedes tend to let it all hang loose. I'm not immediately talking about naturists here, but just losing the control they would have back in their native Sweden. There's nothing remotely different here compared to most Brits going on a

244

summer holiday, but there are still major differences in how they go about it.

When on holiday, Brits will tend to drink, shout, drink and then shout some more. They may drink more than they usually do compared to a night out in their hometown, but most of the time, there is still some kind of boundary that says that they just can't drink anymore. Swedes, on the other hand, will drink themselves into oblivion along with some shouting. At one particular hotel on Gran Canaria, the staff were not pleased when a bunch of Swedes came back late at night, shouting their heads off and not in the best shape. They were almost close to being thrown out at one point, and the cleaning staff had their work cut out for them in the week they were there. Of course, not every Swede or Brit will go on these holidays to drink themselves under the table, and into the closest emergency ward to have their stomach pumped, but it does happen.

Sunny holidays to Gran Canaria also dredge up some people's inhibitions of taking a dip in the sea. The beach is where you will find all kinds of interesting people and the more you observe them, the more interesting or odd they seem to get. Take for example, a conversation I overheard on a beach in Norfolk:

"I really don't care for really hot weather. I just like getting out in the air."

"I agree," said the son.

"You know what?"

"What?"

"When I die, you'll inherit these flip-flops."

The family had so much against hot weather that they had erected a tent and were trying their best to shade themselves completely from the sun. They weren't kidding that they didn't care for hot weather, but actually, this is quite common for Brits to do. Even when travelling abroad. No matter what beach it is, if you see a tent erected, it's probably a British family not wanting to catch the sun. It's slightly bizarre as this is what you pay money for to travel to a sunny beach or so I am led to believe. If you spot children dressed from top to toe in clothes on a warm beach, you can best bet that this is a British child being protected against the sun. Sun tan lotion with factor fifty works. That's all I have to say.

When it comes to Swedes, the complete reverse happens. The fewer clothes you can have on at the beach, the better it is. The more sun a Swede can soak up on these holidays, the better it is. It goes back to making the most of limited sunlight when thinking about the winter months of total darkness.

On the flipside of the coin, Swedes love the cold too, and there is a holiday called *Sportlov* where Swedes will pack up their skiing gear and head for the north. I talked briefly about some businesses

246

shutting down during summer holidays and the same can happen during *Sportlov*. While most of Sweden is on the piste, going up in cable cars, skiing down on snowboards or skis, making snowmen and throwing snowballs in the north, the south can be mostly deserted and appear shut down.

Swedes also have the reputation for travelling and living in other countries but nine times out of ten, they will eventually return to Sweden. There seems to be something about a Swede and their relationship with their home country to want to return to it again like a boomerang. For some, it can be two years, others ten years, even twenty years but Swedes are nearly always magnetised back again.

The Swedish are well known for travelling widely and beyond, but what about people that travel into Sweden on business or for pleasure? Before I moved in 2003, I travelled between the UK and Sweden a number of times, and encountered a surprising number of confused Brits. Travelling for the first time to Sweden can be confusing for some people, but it's never caused me many problems at all after I have landed, unlike two businessmen I was travelling with one time:

"I have no idea how to travel here. I'll just bally well jump on a tram and go!" said the aptly dressed man in a suit and tie.

"Let's follow him! He looks as if he knows what he is doing!" said the other aptly dressed businessman in a similar looking suit and tie.

I turned around and gave a wry smile and decided to try and lose them as quickly as possible. It was up to them to keep up which they promptly didn't do.

Another time that I encountered bewildered English people in Sweden was when I was unlucky to be on a bus journey with about twenty boy scouts. Boy scouts were all about non-baked, good deeds. Helping a granny across the road, tying a knot into a rope (handy for all those knot-tying situations) and sitting around a camp fire singing songs that had clearly been made up by a scout leader that had lost the use of his vocabulary:

- Ging gang gooly gooly whatcha!

- Ging gang goo ging gang goo!

Alongside the campfire tomfoolery, and the good deeds, comes a stigma attached to the poor boy scout. They all seem to have a huge patriotic streak in them, which isn't necessarily a bad thing, but they can take it a little too far by hurling insults and talking loudly about things they know nothing about.

Before I carry on and offend every single boy scout that has existed or exists today, let me throw you this example of the boy scouts on this bus who were sitting behind me, having landed at Gothenburg City Airport, and then you can judge for yourself:

"Oh wow. They have traffic lights here," said the first boy scout, in a quite innocent sounding way.

The others took this occasion to look out of the window. To their disappointment, they just saw fields and large open spaces. Gothenburg City Airport (reported to be closing at the time of writing) is situated on the island of Hisingen, which is quite often mistaken as being the centre of Gothenburg. It's a fairly easy and common mistake to make.

"It's like the third world," said one snotty nosed kid.

"Of course it's the third world, it's not England," said snotty Boy Scout number three, in an equally insulting fashion.

As I sighed heavily and thought of how much they were lowering the perception of English people abroad, they carried on their ill-educated conversation until they got to what they thought was the main central station in the centre of Gothenburg which, in actual fact, was just Hjalmar Brantingsplatsen, a harmless bus stop outside a large number of shops. Looking very confused and disorientated, the scouts started to make prairie dog impressions over the back of the chairs in front of them as the bus came to a stop.

"Is this the main centre?" asked the snotty, third world quote kid, in my direction.

249

"Yeah mate! This is it!" I said, as I saw the whole troop get off at this particular stop, looking pleased with themselves.

Did I feel bad about telling them to get off at the wrong stop? Maybe, but then again I have never been a boy scout so good deeds don't come natural to me, and besides, they were close to the centre. What else could I have done?

Curious Brits, who haven't ventured over to Sweden, will often ask questions to those who have. Is Sweden greener than England? Do they sell fish and chips there? I don't want to take a holiday where it's cold. Is it really cold? It always amazes me when Brits travel to another country, expecting to find British food there as if it is recognised for being the best in the world. To put every Brit's fear to rest, fish and chips are sold in Sweden in English pubs that are inhabited mostly by Brits. If you want to stick to English food then it's your choice to eat it, but you'll miss out on some Swedish dishes that I would try to experience when visiting.

THINGS YOU HAVE LEARNT FROM THIS CHAPTER

• Bears also have trouble standing up on the fast trains.

- Magic roundabouts are banned in Sweden.

- If you want some alone time, take a trip on a Swedish motorway away from a city.

- Illogical road signs don't exist in Sweden.

- There's only fifty miles between Gothenburg and Stockholm.

- Ornamental lemons could be the way forward.

- Swedish ticket inspectors hunt in packs.

- Stockholm buses smell funny.

- "Mind the gap" is a novel in Swedish.

- England has the ability to cut trains in half.

- Calling the name "Svensson" to get the attention of one person will never happen.

- Brits go to sunny places to avoid the sun in tents.

- Who needs town shops when they have their holi days anyway?

- Common sense deserts British tourists on trips to Sweden.

14. WEST vs. EAST

In many countries, the capital cities usually always have a small, harmless war with the next largest city, each claiming that they are better than the other. For example, Gran Canaria and Tenerife always throw sticks at each other when it comes to the best beaches, tourist attractions and clown choirs. You read that right. Clown choirs. Every year, the two islands have competitions featuring a choir dressed up in fancy dress, usually clowns, where they'll sometimes sing songs about how one is better than the other. It's one of the strangest things I have seen but entertaining nevertheless.

Sweden doesn't have any clown choirs singing their hearts out about how good the east or west coasts are because that is left up to the inhabitants of each coastline. In particular, Stockholm and Gothenburg have always had a rivalry with each city trying to outdo the other in the we-are-best stakes. Both cities have the right to do it. Gothenburg might be well known for its laid back, working class humour but does it really stand up against the middle-upper class attitude and beauty of Stockholm? Both have their plus and minus points but is there a clear winner?

CHEWING GUM vs. SNUS

If you have ever been to Stockholm, the first thing you'll be doing is digging a copious amount of chewing gum off your shoes. Unless I have been really unfortunate in treading in every available piece of mouth flung gunk out there, I always come home with at least one blob of it on the sole(s) of my shoes. The closest you'll come to a similar thing happening in Gothenburg is treading on snus that has been sucked dry and thrown on the ground. Just to explain, snus is a cross between chewing tobacco and a teabag, where Swedes force a small pouch under their lip and onto their gum. Instead of sounding like an alien out of *Star Wars* when spitting chewing tobacco out, the empty snus pouch is usually just deposited onto the street. There seems to be more of this going on in Gothenburg compared to Stockholm but I could be wrong. In any case, I would much prefer to walk on a bed of old snus pouches than I would on chewing gum.

CHILLED OUT GOTHENBURGERS vs. BUSY STOCKHOLMERS

The folk in Gothenburg are more chilled out than the folk in Stockholm, despite all the nicotine from the snus consumption. You'll quite often find Gothenburgers cracking one-line jokes, acting like stand-up comics performing a show. Gothenburgers will also tell you that something you have just bought is the best in the whole of Sweden, albeit in a jokey manner. My first purchase of a liquorice ice cream was accompanied with:

"Ha! Ha! Ha! That's a good choice. The best liqourice ice cream in Gothenburg, in Sweden, in the whole world.. Ha! Ha! Ha!"

I couldn't really say whether the ice cream was, in fact, the best of the liquorice variety in the whole world, but I certainly admired the seller's passion for it.

To break the stereotype of every Stockholmer being snobby and stuck-up, I have met some that have been so unbelievably friendly that I have mistaken them for Gothenburgers. You'll usually find the friendly Stockholmer in small, specialist shops who just want you to buy something and leave happy, which you will probably do. However, if you have ever taken time to wander around the Stureplan area, marked on the map by a large, metallic statue of a

255

mushroom, then you'll spot the Stockholmer that has become something of a stereotype. Slick back hair, wrap-around glasses, suit jacket and that's just the women (only joking!). They are usually referred to as a *stekare*. The laid back attitude of the Gothenburger is replaced with the - I-don't-have-time-for-you - attitude instead, with everyone rushing about, trying to get to somewhere. It's nowhere near as busy as London, and if you did collapse on the pavement in Stockholm, the percentage of somebody helping you would be much higher.

SLIDING DOORS

There is, however, one area where the laid back Gothenburg attitude has crept into Stockholm society and in the most infuriating way. Gates and sliding doors open at the speed of a sloth crawling to a new branch. There have been countless times where I have been walking out of tube stations, at my fast pace, only to find my face pressed up against a pane of glass that hasn't got out of my way. Even if you have a monthly travel card, there is a long delay between swiping your card and the gate actually opening, leaving you walking into the gate and injuring yourself. It's a puzzle in Stockholm that I haven't been able to solve as people seem to move quick and be in a rush, and they must surely have encountered the same problem that I have. There have actually been times when doors and gates don't open at all, making me wave to the sensor as if it was a photo opportunity.

Gothenburg has largely escaped automatic doors and gates because they use trams instead of the tube. Both systems work well in either city but there are differences. Gothenburg is cheaper, but you'll have your journey invaded by ticket inspectors whereas Stockholm's tube is much more expensive and has fewer ticket inspectors. Stockholm's tube is considered so expensive that some people just jump the gates and go on their merry way, leaving the person in the control desk to just stare at them as they do it. The Swedish language has the verb *planka* to describe this action and there is also a political movement to support free public transport.

Once you are past the gates, some of Stockholm's tube stations are artworks in themselves with Kungsträdgården's caves being something to behold. Gothenburg, on the other hand, has to rely on the views out of the tram windows. There's nothing wrong with that and both are fairly equal when it comes down to it.

COSY CITY vs. COSMO CITY

Stockholm is a city that you have to keep up with

and not the other way around as is the case with Gothenburg. For example, the Gothenburg Film Festival and Book Fair are both advertised way in advance before it begins, making sure that folk know when it's on. A chunky catalogue is produced to further enhance the potential visitor's knowledge before paying for something that they don't like. It's unlikely that someone won't find something that they don't like at either event because they attract some big names in the world of film and literature. When an event happens in Gothenburg, everybody knows about it and has to take part. In Stockholm, it's more likely you'll spot an old advert on the tube stating when the film festival happened and the fact that you missed it. The chunky catalogues are hard to find, and there aren't any street banners or posters advertising it until it is too late. It's nothing personal, but Stockholm just assumes that you already know when these things are happening. It also happens with other events, which will lead the average mortal man to believe that Stockholm has an attitude of - we are the capital and don't have to try hard - compared to Gothenburg's - Ha! Ha! Ha! It's a good decision to come to both the film and book fairs. The best events in Gothenburg. In Sweden. In the whole entire world. Ha! Ha! Ha!

Stockholm is known as the Venice of the north because of its beautiful buildings, waterways and coastal scenery. It has a heap of tourist attractions like Skansen, an open air museum, Gröna Lund, a theme park, Vasa, a museum dedicated to a restored

17th century ship and Gamla Stan (old town) to be reckoned with. Gothenburg may not have those things but it does have: Slottskogen, a cost free challenger to Skansen; Liseberg, well considered to beat Gröna Lund hands down; Haga, a contender that tries to beat Gamla Stan but it has no chance really and The East Indiaman replica project to rival Vasa, where both have their own charms but maybe Vasa, being the real McCoy, wins here, although East Indiaman is very, very close.

Gothenburg may not be compared to Venice, but it does have the nickname little London. There aren't many similarities to be found. London has the Thames; Gothenburg has a canal. London has the tube and double decker buses; Gothenburg has trams and single deckers. London has the London Eye; Gothenburg doesn't... wait! It does have the Gothenburg Wheel. It rains a lot in London; it rains a lot in Gothenburg.

Even though Gothenburg is more industrial than Stockholm, both cities offer escapes through boat trips to islands located on the west and east coasts. A journey by boat out to an island from Gothenburg is still beautiful but in a different way compared to Stockholm. Stockholm may have the fancy buildings, swanky on-the-water cafés and restaurants, but Gothenburg has the Opera House, situated on the waterfront, Eriksborg Fortress, and the landmark Lipstick building.

259

CONSTRUCTION

Gothenburg and Stockholm are constant victims to change and construction work is to be expected. Stockholm is always being modernised to keep it looking up to date whereas the roads in Gothenburg always seem to be under constant maintenance. It almost bears a resemblance to my hometown where the local council seem to dig a hole in the middle of the road without a good reason. It's as if the city planners have their meetings, alongside their gourmet tea and choccy biccies, open a box of pins, don some blindfolds, and aimlessly stab a pin into a map of my hometown. Whoever stabs the best pin into the map is where a hole will be dug. I liken this to the childhood game of 'pin the tail on the donkey', but is called 'let's make a bloody big hole in the road' instead.

At the end of the day, Stockholmers are very proud to be just that. You'll rarely find a Stockholmer that will prefer Gothenburg to the capital and the same can be said vice versa. So who wins when one of them mouths off? The answer? Nobody wins. Just visit both and enjoy.

THINGS YOU HAVE LEARNT FROM THIS CHAPTER

- Bears have no preference to Stockholm or Gothenburg.

- Your feet might stick to the pavement in Stockholm.

- Gothenburg pavements are padded.

- Everybody is a comedian in Gothenburg.

- Smack! That gate in Stockholm will eventually open.

- Don't *planka*. It'll just raise the prices for every other law-abiding citizen.

- Missed the Stockholm Film Festival? So has everyone else.

- Northampton will never be finished so long as council workers have a fresh supply of choccie biccies.

- If a Gothenburger is criticising Stockholm or vice versa, ignore them. They are both wrong.

15. COUNTRY & ENVIRONMENT

It was hard to know what to expect when I first visited Sweden. A part of me expected to see Swiss like scenery from *A Sound of Music*—wide-open spaces with rolling green fields but without the nuns and Julie Andrews getting into the picture. The only other part of Sweden I had seen were rally cars slipping and sliding their way to the finish line in sleet and snow. Neither of these descriptions is that far wrong, as forests and lakes cover the majority of Sweden.

LAKES AND FORESTS

To have so many lakes is an advantage for the outdoorsy, swim-loving Swede who just can't wait to take a dip as soon as the sun has projected its first ray nearing the summer. As beautiful as the lakes are and as picture perfect as the surroundings are, if you closed your eyes, took a mystery tour to any lake in

Sweden and then opened them, it would be hard to know whereabouts in the country you were because one lake is pretty much like the other.

Then again, there are small lakes and then there's Vänern, the largest lake in Sweden, which is so large that you would easily assume it to be the sea.

The forests, on the other hand, could contribute to why the air in Sweden is so clear and fresh. When I first visited back in 2002, I encountered a few surprises.

Not being able to smell and breathe in exhaust fumes.

The sky wasn't grey.

The lakes and seas were actually blue.

The air felt healthy and, somehow, crisper.

It took some getting used to.

When I eventually moved to a suburb of Gothenburg in 2003, I relocated to an area that was immersed in forest, which really became my back garden. It made a change not to live on a busy road and hear heavy goods vehicles thunder past at any given hour. In some ways, I had no idea what effect being kept subliminally awake was doing to me and it became apparent after my very first week of living in Gothenburg. Gone were the days of that trail bike going up and down the road, umpteen times a day. Gone were the days of drunks shouting and singing their way home past my bedroom window. Gone were the days of waking up in the night, wondering what that noise had been. None of that had happened because of one factor – it was just too damn quiet.

In my first week of living in Gothenburg, I was amazed when I woke up at 2 p.m. in the afternoon. A rub of the eyes, a look at the clock, another rub of the eyes. No way! 2 p.m.? It had never been in my nature to wake up that late, not even if I had been drinking the night before and my head felt as if it had been smacked heavily with a mallet, and had breath as deadly as mustard gas. Living near, or in, a forest certainly had its advantages, and the only chance of me being disturbed in my sleep would have been an irate squirrel that was having trouble with a stubborn nut.

THE COUNTRY HOUSE

What effect has the amount of forest and open land had on the locals who live in these areas? In Sweden, I have only lived in the cities of Gothenburg and Stockholm, but there was a time when I spent a few days in the country, staying with my girlfriend's parents while she was in hospital recovering from an extreme case of food poisoning. The first problem about living in a remote part of Sweden is that there is very little to do and although living in the country is certainly therapeutic, cabin fever is likely to strike any city slicker trying to live there. After I had settled into my new temporary abode, I tried to entertain myself with some TV but couldn't deduce how the satellite channels worked and after fiddling with the remote, I eventually gave up. Twiddling my thumbs only entertained me for a short, until I made the decision to go outside and walk around with my camera.

I had been told to not let any of the fourteen cats waiting outside into the house on account of the fact that my girlfriend's dad was allergic to them. Bearing this in mind, I inched the back door open only to leave a gap large enough to let cats through. Quickly realising my mistake, I was, unfortunately, not as quick in shutting the door because the cats were invading the house.

Woosh.

One cat.

Woosh.

Two cats.

Woosh.

Three cats.

I closed the back door to the cats' only entrance to the house. I then had to deal with the trio that had made their dash into the warm, inviting cosiness of the house. The first cat to be caught and subsequently thrown out was easy because it had stopped and cowed down beside my feet expecting it to happen.

One down, two to go.

Coming to the realisation that a large, three-level house was going to hamper my attempts in every respect, I managed to find the next cat in a bedroom. It didn't go quietly and escaped my clutches. After an hour's chase across all the rooms of the house, some of which I was sure I hadn't seen before as even standard Swedish houses are fiendishly large, the cat was eventually cornered, caught and thrown out.

Two down, one to go.

The third cat was a serious problem. I could tell what floor it had made its way onto because of the noisy meows it was making, but actually finding out where it was hiding was more of a mystery. After a while of scratching my head and not being able to localise it, I gave up. My girlfriend's dad would have to put up with sneezing and coughing until it showed itself.

Why the elaborate cat story? Well, this was really the only entertainment I had being in a house with no TV or computer, an outside world where there were only trees and not a lot else, and only having a camera to keep myself occupied. If this situation ever happens to you, my advice is to open the back door and hope for some form of entertainment to come through it.

If you find yourself in the sticks in the wintertime and everything is frozen solid, you can always try to entertain yourself by trying to build a snowman, but as much as you want to go outside, the freezing temperatures will almost certainly scare you back in for a warm cup of soup.

FLIES

On the other hand, if you venture outside in the summertime, you would have thought the sunlight and scenery would just be stunning. In most respects it is but for one problem. Flies. As soon as you stick your head outside the front door, a grey cloud of circling flies will be visible above you even though you remembered to shower that day. Trying to ignore the flies will become impossible because the more you walk outside, the more they'll try anything to enter your body, for some reason, through any orifice that is not covered up. They'll try your ears first just to make you jump, and then try your nose, and then your mouth, obviously hoping for some kind of egg laying opportunity. You'll soon know how farmyard animals feel as you wave your hands around in semaphores, trying to bat the buzzing annoyances away. By the time you have got five minutes down the road, you'll have come to the conclusion that staying home is the best idea after all. But this only seems to happen in wild open countryside when compared to city parks and nature trails.

PARKS

In both Gothenburg and Stockholm, the powers that be have devoted a fair amount of space to parks. The first one that I visited was called Slottskogen in Gothenburg. Slottskogen, which translated means castle forest, boasts lakes, a volleyball park and penguins. Yep. Penguins. As unusual as I thought it was to see a sign pointing to penguins, I couldn't resist checking it out. The sign did indeed confirm my suspicion of penguins, thirty of them, packed in a small room with two pelicans that seemed agitated about being locked up with them. The pelicans were inclined to show that agitation by flapping their wings at various intervals, sending a good number of penguins for their first flight towards the glass of their cramped dwellings.

An urban myth about a man who kidnapped, or rather penguinnapped, a penguin from Slottskogen has circulated through the city since time began. Apparently, a drunk man on his way home thought it would be a great idea to take a penguin from the park home with him. When he woke up the following morning, there was a penguin flapping around in his bathtub asking for a sponge and some shower gel. You can probably assume this story is false but it doesn't avoid it being told by many Gothenburgers.

The equivalent in Stockholm is called Skansen, where they thought it was a good idea to up-root whole buildings, anything from small cabins to church steeples, from all over the country and put them all in the capital. This is a slightly eccentric idea, but most Swedes obviously thought it was a good idea to preserve the country's assets.

Both parks have animals aplenty that don't have attitude problems (apart from that bear I tried to take a photo of) to gawp at and both have an un-canny knack of making you feel that you are not in a city. Try as you might, it's hard to hear any traffic noise in these parks and it makes me wonder how they achieved it. When compared to my hometown, these parks seemed like completely different univers-es entirely. Most of the parks and nature trails in my hometown hit the headlines for a variety of different reasons: attacks, perverts, scouts.

DAYLIGHT vs. DUSK

Nothing in the land of Swedonia affects people more than day versus night. When the summer months start to get closer and closer, Swedes are bit-ing their fingernails, wiggling their legs and gritting their teeth in anticipation of the first dip in a lake or sea. Nothing charges up a Swede more than the chance to go to their summer home, often known as a sommarstuga, when midsummer gets closer.

The daylight gets to a point where in the north, above the Arctic Circle, where the sun doesn't set at all. 24-hour sun. You heard me. The closest I have come to 24-hour sun was in Östersund. Even though it's far from the Arctic Circle, if you are out on the town at 11 p.m. and come out at 5 a.m., it will still look like daytime. Nothing screws with a human brain more than this. I certainly couldn't figure it out and thought to myself:

Now hold on a minute. Is there something wrong with my watch? Is it time for breakfast or should that be brunch?

I then started to think it must be way past lunch. I made up new terms like 'linner' or 'dunch' to try and fit my meals into what the daylight was dictating. The mere fact that I was talking gibberish also hammered home the fact that I couldn't handle 24-hour daylight.

24-hour daylight is to make up for the dreadful lack of it towards Christmas time where the same northern cities and towns get bugger all daylight. If you live in Sweden, you'll have to get used the fact that people will be coming up to you saying:

- God! I feel tired.

271

- I don't know what's wrong with me.

- I got enough sleep last night but still feel zonked.

If one way of solving this problem is suicide then I will just point out how illogical that sounds. It's like saying:

- Well, I'm depressed with this 24-hour darkness. I know what. I'll just make it permanent 24-hour darkness instead. That'll solve the problem.

Sure, it's a bit dreary when it's dark, and you can put your frozen vegetables out on the balcony instead of in the freezer, but suicide is not the answer!

So now you know what to expect when you come to Sweden. Sweeping landscapes, mountains and lakes. You get all of those things as long as you make the most of the daylight because, post August, it all gets a bit darker and colder.

THINGS YOU HAVE LEARNT FROM THIS CHAPTER

- You might meet a bear in the countryside but it won't be as humanlike as the Skansen variety.

- Country cats are entertainment.

- Flies want to get personal with you.

- Penguins and pelicans don't mix.

- Penguinnapping doesn't pay.

- 24-hour sunlight can screw up breakfast, brunch, dunch and linner.

- Darker days make people grumpy.

16. CONCLUSION or WHAT YOU SHOULD HAVE LEARNT BY READING THIS BOOK.

Well done. You made it to this part of the book. The end. Well, almost the end. You have to actually read this chapter wannabe right to last bitter full stop. This is the epilogue that ties up all the chapters into one bite size slice, and will bring to a conclusion what I have learnt and more importantly what you have learnt too.

In my ten years in Sweden, the most important thing I have learnt is to take advantage of the free education system, as this will pay dividends. Signing up to free Swedish lessons is really worthwhile if you want to get ahead in Sweden, despite the fact that you might have to listen to bongos, wave your arms around in circles, and look at a teacher with a red sock on their hand.

This, in turn, may well find you a job. If you manage to do this then you have really cracked Sweden. You'll find that even though the taxman takes more out of your wage, you should have more left over at the end of the day depending on what job you get. Once you have got that all important first job in Sweden, then the next best thing you can do is get yourself paying into an a-kassa & union membership, as this will offer up benefits aplenty if you decide to study or set up your own business.

The equivalent to your national insurance number should be the first thing you should register for if you are considering moving, and an ID card will also come in very handy too.

That's the serious stuff out of the way.

I have also learnt that asking people how much they have bought something for is a big no-no and could be taken as an insult. I have come to the realisation that Swedes try their best to live in a society where everyone is fairly equal, and I leave money matters out of general conversations altogether.

Little things like turning up to meetings on time, making sure bar codes face away from the cashier, and keeping calm at music concerts all have to be mastered at some point in time although it might go against your Britishness.

When speaking to a Swede, and they are using words that sound like swearwords, just do your best to gloss over them and don't take it personally. They probably weren't swearing at you in the first place and, in actual fact, probably like you instead.

The stereotypes of the Swedish chef, nudists, and that all Swedes have blonde hair, blue eyes and are beautiful have largely been busted in this book. Nobody sounds like the Swedish chef, nudists exist but are in small supply, and not everyone has blonde hair and blue eyes although Swedes do have the knack of being blessed with beauty.

The deer and magpies in Sweden are tamer when compared to the UK. This could be due to Swedes being non-threatening. It's hardly surprising when the country has been peaceful and not involved in any wars for a couple of centuries. This leaves the wildlife with a - whatever - attitude that will just have them ignoring humans completely while they munch on the natural vegetation.

If you are a Brit, you will cringe at sing-a-long shows on TV and will not have a clue why traditional songs will join all Swedes together. Dansband will look as if hundreds of Showaddywaddy tribute bands have come out of retirement, and if you are a musician, H might be mentioned as a musical note.

Tackling food could be considered a health hazard while your taste buds are subjected to Kalles Kaviar, but might be rewarded if you get through the sulfurous whiff of *surströmming*. Shrimps don't yield much meat but at least they are easier to peel than the Rubik's cube of the deep, the crayfish.

Public transport may run on time and be fairly easy to pay for, but this doesn't stop a large number of confused British tourists getting on planes, buses and trams asking me questions about it.

So, is Sweden a better place to live when compared to my hometown of Northampton? In my opinion, the answer to this question is yes. Living standards are generally higher, and Northampton will never be able to offer me a sea view and a fresh plate of seafood. Getting a job and learning the language might be hard and send some Brits back home with their heads down, but if you are willing to take advantage of the free education, you might just make it through the long haul.

There are obviously some elements of Northampton and the UK that I miss—mostly old friends and family who can never be replaced. Other than this, I don't regret moving to Sweden, and have never taken the beauty of the country for granted.

APPENDIX

THE BASTARDISED SWEDISH TO ENGLISH DICTIONARY.

There are some words that sound funny in Swedish to English people. There are some words that translate badly to English if directly translated from Swedish. What follows is a collection, a small dictionary if you will, of translated Swedish words directly into English and then what they mean in reality. Thanks to everyone who helped compile this list.

Words

bajskorv – poo sausage - turd

bajsvatten - poo water - sewage

berg- och dalbana – mountain and valley track - rollercoaster blindtarm - blind intestine - appendix

blixtlås – flash lock - zip

björntjänst - bear service - disservice

brudnäbb - bride beak - page girl

bröstvårta – breast wart - nipple

bärfis - berry fart - shield beetle

dammsugare – dust sucker - vacuum cleaner

domstol – verdict chair - court

dragkedja – pull chain - zip

dragplåster - pull plaster - big attraction

dragspel - pull play - accordion

ett ögonblick - one eye look - one moment

fladdermus – flap mouse - bat

fläskberg – pork mountain - fat person or someone who is porky

försöksdjur – try animal – guinea pig (e.g a lab rat)

grönsaker – green things - vegetables

godisgris – sweet pig - sweet tooth

gnällspik – whining nail - a person who whines a lot

halsmandlar – throat almonds - tonsils

hedersprick – honour dot – honourable guy

hejduk - hello cloth - henchman

härmapa – mimic monkey - mimic

inhoppare – in jumper - substitute

jordekorre - earth squirrel - chipmunk

jordgubbar – earth old men - strawberries

kofot – cow foot – crow bar – kråkpinne

korvstoppning - sausage stuffing - cramming (for an exam)

kärringstopp – hag stop - to stall a car ("stalled it!")

liktorn - corpse tower - Corn (on your feet)

lipsill – cry herring - person that cries a lot

läckergom – delicious palate - gourmet

lårkaka - thigh cake - burst thigh muscle

mansgris – man pig - male chauvinist

munspel - mouth play – harmonica

olycksfågel – accident bird - someone who is unlucky all the time

parhäst - pair horse - sidekick - sida spark

påssjuka – bag sickness - mumps

rackabajsare - rascal pooer - a hard shot in sport and drinks

skavfötter – chafe feet – lie head to foot

språkgroda - language frog - malapropism

snorkråkor – snot crows - bogies

snuskhummer – filth lobster - pervert

snöbyar - snow villages - snow showers

smörgås – butter goose - open sandwich

smaklökar – taste onions – taste buds – smakknoppar

solkatt – sun cat - sun spot

skitstövlar – shit boots - bastards

skit samma – shit the same - never mind

skitbra – shit good - really good

svartsjuk – black sick - jealous

struphuvud – throat head - larynx

sugrör – suck pipe - straw

skitungar – shit kids - bloody kids

ståhej – stand hello – hullabaloo

tandtroll – tooth troll - it is the reverse of the tooth fairy that gives you cavaties

tandkött – tooth meat - gums

tuggummi – chew rubber - chewing gum

tvättbjörn - wash bear - raccoon

underlivet – the under life - the genitals

våghals - dare throat - dare devil

väderspänningar - weather tensions - flatulence

Others

bena ut – bone out – analyse

hajar du? - do you shark? - do you understand?

han är en riktig torsk - he is a real cod - he is a punter (for prostitutes)

jag är gift – I am poison(ed) - I am married

klämma i sig – squeeze in yourself – eat something all at once

se upp – see up – watch out

skjuta upp – shoot up – postpone

slå upp böckerna! – beat up the books – open the books

spöka ut sig – ghost out yourself – overdress (often in a crazy way)

ta en tupplur – take a cock nap – take a nap

varm korv med bröd – warm sausage with bread – hot dog – varm hund – warm dog

Small Phrases

Now, when it comes to phrases, England has some real gems. For example, "it's raining cats and dogs" is a prime example. However, Swedes have not escaped using phrases either and they crop up in conversation leaving immigrants asking "what exactly did that mean?" The following is a small list of some phrases in Sweden.

Att bära hundhuvudet – to carry the dog head – to become a scapegoat

Den gubben går inte – that old man doesn't walk - that story will not do

Det är inte mitt bord – it's not my table – it's not my responsibility

Det är ingen ko på isen, så länge rumpan är i land – there's no cow on the ice, so long as the bum is on land – there's nothing to worry about

Din lyckans ost - your cheese of happiness - you lucky person!

Fastna med skägget i brevlådan – to get caught with the beard in the letter box – to get yourself in a sticky situation

Få korgen – get the basket – to be dumped (in a relationship)

Ge igen för gammal ost – give again for old cheese – to avenge a wrong

Glida in på en räkmacka – glide in on a shrimp sandwich – to get everything without trying

Gå på i ullstrumporna – to walk in woolly socks – to carry on regardless

Går åt skogen – goes to the forest – things are going wrong

Göra en pudel – make a poodle – to make a humble apology after first denying your mistake

Ha rent mjöl i påsen – have clean flour in the bag – to be honest

Har inte alla hästar hemma – has not all the horses at home – someone who's not so clever

Jag anar ugglor i mossen – I suspect owls in the bog - something is a bit fishy

Jag har klippt mig – I have cut myself - I have had a haircut

Jag har släppt mig – I have released myself - I have passed wind

Köpa grisen i säcken – buy the pig in the sack - buy something unseen

Kan du skruva upp volymen på radion? – can you screw up the volume on the radio? – can you turn up the volume on the radio?

Koka soppa på en spik – cook soup on a nail – to cook with minimum ingredients

Komma på grön kvist – to get on a green twig – to improve your finances after hardship

Lika goda kålsupare – just as good cabbage sippers – It's not better than the other

Mumla i skägget – mumble in the beard – to not speak clearly

Någonting i hästväg – something in horse way – something is a spectacularly big

Odla sin kål – cultivate one's cabbage – to concentrate on your own private projects

Nu ska du få se på andra bullar – now you will see other buns – there are going to be some changes made here

Pang på rödbetan – bang on the beetroot - to the point

Pudelns kärna – the poodle's core – the root of the problem

Sitta hemma och uggla – sit at home and owl – to watch paint dry

Sitta på pottkanten – to sit on the pot edge – to put in a spot or up against the wall

Skita i det blå skåpet – to shit in the blue cupboard – to give yourself away or embarrass yourself

Skit på dig – shit on yourself - go screw yourself

Sjutton också – 17 also - shhhhh… sugar (saying sugar instead of shit)

Slå sina påsar ihop – put one's bags together – to get married or work together

Sy in dem – sew them in - lock them up (in jail)

Vad håller du på med? – what are you holding on with? – what are you playing at? (said angrily) what are you doing? (said nicely)

Vi har soppatorsk – we have soup cod – we have run out of petrol

TV and Film Translations

Sometimes, TV and film titles are changed for the Swedish public. Sometimes it is for their own good as some titles can't be easily understood. However, there are times when translated film titles and characters could have been left as they were as you'll quickly realise by reading the examples below.

Agent 007 ser rött – Agent 007 sees red – From Russia With Love

Ett päron till farsa på semester i Europa – A pear of a father in holiday in Europe - National Lampoon's

European Vacation

Helan och halvan – the whole and the half - Laurel and Hardy

Karl Alfred – Popeye

Läderlappen – The leather note - Batman

Långben – long legs - The Disney character Goofy

Pantertanter – The panther old women - The Golden Girls

Snobbar som jobbar – snobs who work – The Persuaders

Stackars Dennis – Poor Dennis - Jabberwocky

Stjärnor utan hjärnor – stars without brains - Jay and Silent Bob

Fart Words

The Swedish language uses the word fart which will always raise a wry smile to native English speakers, childish as it is. Fart in Swedish actually means speed although it appears in compound words. Here are just some of the fart words to have a giggle at:

Infart

Utfart

Uppfart

Lastinfart

I full fart

Fartkamera

Farthinder

Fartyget

Fartfylld

Fartsyndare

Fartkontroll

Fartgräns

Fartblind

Fartdåre

Fartpolis

Snigelfart

Swedes have their own small giggle at the expense of the Fédération Internationale de Ski, which is abbreviated to FIS, the Swedish word for fart.

Swedish Words That Are Spelt Like English Words

There are times when Swedish words can mean something in English like the aforementioned fart. Slut is often pointed out by fellow Brits as being obviously funny but there are so many other words that, perhaps, are overlooked once Swedish has been learnt to a good standard. Here are just a few of them:

barnet – the child

block – writing pad

bra – good

dog – died

dragon – tarragon

fast – stuck

fukt – damp and moisture

fårskinn – sheepskin (somebody I knew mistook fårskinn for foreskin. Don't worry that sheepskin jacket you like the look of is not made out of foreskins.)

get – goat

gift – poison or married

hat – hate

hit – here (e.g. here in this direction)

hot – threat

i morgon bitti – early in the morning (only funny if you have watched Little Britain)

kiss – pee

kock – chef

käck – bright or lively (not pronounced cack just in case you are wondering)

list – skirting board

medges – is allowed or permitted (looks like it should be pronounced the same as wedges but it's not so don't attempt it)

men – but

mucka – to finish military service or to pick a fight

mums – yum yum

nobba – to turn somebody / something down

nobless – nobility (sorry! Doesn't mean eunuch!)

pant – deposit

pippa – to have sex (this is a harmless nickname for someone called Phillipa)

prick – spot

puss – kiss (you don't want to get these two mixed up)

randig – stripy (it sounds like the word randy)

rap - burp

river – tears (e.g tears down something)

rot – root

sin – his, hers, its, theirs

skum – foam

slag – beat / strike

slipper – avoids or gets out of doing something

slump – chance

slut – end

snack - chat

spott – spit

spring – run

spy – vomit (there is a well-known bar in Stockholm called Spy Bar. I sure hope they mean spy in the English sense because it'll put a lot of people off if not)

stick – sting / disappear

stolen – the chair

suck - sigh

teet – the tea

trots att – despite (not as in "got a touch of the trots")

(träd)huggare (official word: skogshuggare) – lumberjack (the word trädhuggare doesn't actually exist in dictionaries but doesn't stop some Swedes from using it. When I heard someone say this word I thought they had said tree hugger. It doesn't mean they are a tree hugger, quite the reverse.)

English Words

This section would not be complete without some form of revenge taken for the Swedes looking in on the English language. So just for them, here are some bastardisations of English words directly translated to Swedish and then what they really mean.

As rare as hen's teeth – lika ovanlig som hönständer – någonting väldigt ovanligt

Deadline – död linje - tidsgräns

Fireworks – eldarbeten - fyrverkeri

It doesn't cut the mustard – det skär inte senapen – någonting som inte är bra nog

Makes my teeth itch – får mina tänder att klia – någonting som irriterar någon mycket

Partypooper – festbajsare - någon som sabbar en fest

Slow coach – långsam buss - någon som är långsam

Sticky wicket - kladdig grind - svårt situation

The bee's knees – biets knä - någon som är bäst på någonting

The dog's bollocks – hundans pung - någonting som är jättebra (t.ex this car is the dog's bollocks)

The pot calling the kettle black – grytan kallar vattenkokaren svart - någon säger att någon är skyldig när han/hon själv är skyldig

The wrong end of the stick – fel end av pinnen – någon som har missförstått någonting

To flog a dead horse – att prygla en död häst – slå in öppna dörrar